Tejas Kale

Beyond Infinity

TO MOM & DAD

"For constantly encouraging me to give my best inputs"

Editing by Tejas kale

Editing by Yash S Aparajit

Cover art by Yash S Aparajit

Introduction (Book 2) Beyond Infinity

As in the previous book we learned several ethics and the working of the universe. The formation of the solar system, stars, and planets to the constellations and star patterns. Book 1 (Void to Infinity) was the general idea behind terms astronomy and space science.

We all are here as a whole to get more knowledge about the vast universe. The human interest in space is fascinating and enduring. We can drive the hypothetical questions and answers in well-explained terms and it continues to the realm of space and time. We have to use imagination along with intelligence in accordance to understand the universe in many aspects.

Discoveries in Cosmology can raise mankind to greater heights. It will have great significance and intellect at particular times. In this book, you will be forced to reveal the truth of the universe and you will be able to think apart from daily stuff. The invincible curiosity and exploration have provided benefits to our society to study the cosmos from a closer level.

Today we can have the key to the universe and the later generations can join this exciting journey and contribute their presence in studying astronomy. Today it is a challenge for all of us to go deeper into space and carry on the exploration and study cosmos, and surely this era can have a beautiful end. And the space tech generations will now take over the curiosity and will have a well-defined path to have a brighter and more vast future in space technology. Book 2 will take you deep into the cosmos. Beyond Infinity will provide a brief idea of working and explain the complex terms in simple terms including the equations.

Preface

"The Universe will always be considered as next level extraordinary platform to show unusual and curious happenings that will be known in recurring decades" this is how author feels the universe. The terms space, universe and cosmology are always fascinating for the author. From childhood itself he started exploring space-related facts and conquered many more of the same. The author always believes in enhancing knowledge by sharing it. With the same idea of sharing the knowledge he wrote his first book "VOID TO INFINITY" as co-author. And this is second book "BEYOND INFINITY". Author believes in "" thought of   which made him to write his book in very simple language. The language is completely understandable for one who does not have any prior knowledge about space. The reader will have deep dive into the knowledge of space while reading the book. Book includes many terms like...which make reader feel close to the universe.

The author will always be grateful for everyone who adds value to his journey.

Acknowledgement

First, I would like to express my gratitude towards field of Cosmology, for unlocking my perspectives towards fundamentals of universe. I would also like to thank my sister "Ashwini Kale" & "Arati Aher" for constantly making me believe in my dreams. sincere thanks to my brother-in-law "Kishor Aher" because I believe his guidance has led to a significant change in my work ethic, career goals and general outlook.

I would like to extend my gratitude towards my mentor "Kiran Kadam" for guiding me throughout the process. I am writing to thank you for your valuable mentoring over the last two years. It's hard to express how important our partnership has been to my career development.

Appendix

Void to Infinity

In the previous book, we learn about the working and formation of the solar system and our universe. And how our planets are formed to learn the common working of the universe.

Big Bang

The big bang word itself makes a ton of sense as we know the big bang means a large boom / a large burst of something etc. The universe in which we live was also created with a big bang. It is said to be unimaginably hot when the bang happened. When the big bang took place, it was an incredible burst of expansion known to be inflation, in which space expanded faster than the speed of light. It is said that the big bang universe doubled by size at least 90 times, from subatomic size to golf-ball-sized almost in a few milliseconds. All of this data about the big bang and the universe's expansion is the work of great astronomers. But they could not explain or couldn't prove direct evidence for some stuff, such as the gravitational waves associated with the cosmic microwave background or the radiation from the big bang. Cosmic microwave background was in existence from the time of the big bang. It also hurts gravitational waves. This helps us in understanding the beginning of the universe and it is considered that the cosmic microwave background waves are still present in the vast universe by that we can learn several factors and aspects of gravitational waves.

According to NASA [The National Aeronautics and Space Administration], after inflation, the growth of the universe continued but passively. And as it expanded it cooled and matter formed. The seconds after the big bang the universe was growing passively and as well as was filled with neutrons, protons, electrons, anti-electrons, photons, and neutrinos. In the first three minutes, the light elements were born in a 4 THE BIG BANG process known as big bang nucleosynthesis. There was also no existence of time at the time of the big band, all the stuff was inside a small point source which later on is considered as a big bang. At this point, the universe came into existence and spread in all possible directions along with all the higher dimensions. All the atoms and subatomic particles started to attract to each other to have a bond with each other. Then the universe cooled and protons and neutrons collided to make deuterium, an isotope of hydrogen, and combined well again to make helium and lithium in small quantities. We will study cosmic microwave background radiation in the advanced study of the universe. But after that point universe was plunged into darkness as no stars had been formed yet.

Then after that, all the hydrogen atoms started to attract with each other with the help of gravity to form higher-order mass stars and subatomic particles. All these hydrogen atoms got involved in complex reactions that are not defined in the big bang theory. And a little after 9 billion years after the Big Bang our solar system was born. So, it can be said the big bang was full of mysteries, and tons of things are still to be found and explained but as we advance as humans, we will be finding new and advanced ways to find answers to a lot of questions. An amazing fact about this is universe could be as old as 13.8 billion years but our solar system is only 4.6 billion years old. The big bang did create our universe but there are still mysteries covering a ton of information about the genesis of the infinitely big universe from dark matter to the cosmic microwave background and even the case of the gravitational waves associated with it. This is the general idea behind the big bang and how it takes place, this is the most important foundation of all time.

Creation of Solar System.

Our solar system is one of the most beautiful systems in the universe. We know it consists of 8 planets, a ton of moons and asteroids as well as dwarf planets but we don't know how was our solar system created and how many years it took from the big bang. Let's see the creation of our solar system from the start.

Our solar system was formed bout 4.6 billion years ago from a dense cloud of interstellar gas and dust. The cloud collapsed, possibly due to the shockwave of a nearby exploding star, called a supernova. At the center of the super nebula, gravity pulled a ton of materials that eventually increased the pressure in the core causing the hydrogen atoms to combine and form helium and releasing a tremendous amount of energy. This release of energy made our Sun. After the birth of the Sun, it amassed up all the available matter and the matter farther out in the disk was also clumping together as the sun's gravity increased.

These clumps of matter smashed into one another, forming larger and larger objects or so-called cosmic entities. Some of those cosmic entities grew bigger and through their gravity shaped them into spheres, becoming planets, dwarf planets, and large moons. And all the other leftovers could not come together and made the asteroids, comets, meteoroids, and small moons. The solar system was created like this isn't this amazing that after the sun was created the gravity of the sun cause the genesis of all the planets, moons, and all the different asteroids, comets, and meteoroids?

The planets near the sun where need to be able to withstand a ton of heat when the solar system was young so the remains of rocky materials were only able to do so, so these rocky clumps of materials made our first four planets – Mercury, Venus, Earth and Mars which are also known as the terrestrial planets. All these planets were small with a solid, rocky surface that could withstand heat and solar storms. While, all the other elements we are used to seeing like ice, liquid, or gases settled in the outer region of the solar system. The gravity created by all of this matter caused the creation of the gas giants Jupiter and Saturn and Ice giants Uranus and Neptune.

Now I know you would like to mention Pluto, yes Pluto was considered the last planet or the 9th planet in our solar system but when the questions were raised by the IAU [The International Astronomical Union] what were the criteria to be taken to denote planets a full-sized planet and not a dwarf planet it was cleared that as I quote,"

It should be in orbit around the sun, It, should have sufficient mass to assume hydrostatic equilibrium (Roughly round shape) and cleared the neighborhood around its orbit" but Pluto did meet one of these standards for becoming a full-sized planet so the category of the dwarf planets was the only place it could go.

Moreover, more cosmic structures could be added to the list and now the count of these dwarf planets ranges from 5 to 110 but the 5 best-known dwarf planets are Ceres, Pluto, Makemake, Haumea, and Eris.

How Life formed on Earth

Now as we go on let's learn about how life took place on Earth. Yes, live the building blocks of everything we see on earth from plants and animals to us humans. To explain the evolution of life on earth there are many theories but the most popular theories are, "The RNA Theory" and "The Oparin-Haldane Hypothesis", so, we will be having a deep dive into both of these theories. So, let's start.

The RNA theory has suggested a scenario that some 4.47 billion years ago, only 60 million years after Earth took shape and 40 million years after the moon formed a big cosmic entity with the size same as the moon sideswiped Earth and exploded into an orbiting cloud of molten iron and other debris. The metallic hailstorm that formed lasted for years, ripping oxygen atoms from water molecules and leaving hydrogen behind. The oxygen was then free to link with iron, creating vast rust-colored deposits of iron oxide across our planet's surface. The hydrogen formed a dense atmosphere that likely lasted 200 million years as it ever so slowly dissipated into space.

After everything cooled, simple organic molecules began to form under the blanket of hydrogen. Those molecules, as some scientists think, eventually linked up to form RNA, a molecular player long credited as essential for life's dawn. And thus, it was ruled as the theory that can be used for the evolution of life on earth. This theory is still not fully accepted by scientists but can be a candidate in the race of theories for the evolution of life questions. That was all about the RNA theory but it is still not clear how would have RNA jump-started life on earth, if you don't understand how - check this out RNA is a complex molecule and is called Ribonucleic Acid. It is a polymeric molecule essential in the biological coding, decoding, regulating, and expression of genes. So, scientists think via the RNA theory that life started when hydrogen molecules linked up somehow and created RNA, and then life began. But they are a lot of questions like how somehow hydrogen link can create a complex RNA molecule. And yes, it's true but there are no answers.

Oparin-Haldane Hypothesis

So now let's check another path a way that can make some sense to the evolution or to say the origin of life on earth "The Oparin-Haldane Hypothesis". Let's jump in. In the 1920s, Russian scientist Aleksandr Oparin and English scientist J. B. S. Haldane both separately proposed what's now called the Oparin-Haldane hypothesis, that life on Earth could have arisen step-by-step from non-living matter through a process of "gradual chemical evolution." Yes, gradual chemical evolution, means chemical changes on the primitive Earth that gave rise to the first forms of life.

Oparin and Haldane thought that the early Earth had a reducing atmosphere, meaning an oxygen-poor atmosphere in which molecules tend to donate electrons. Suggesting that simple inorganic molecules could have reacted with the energy from lightning or the sun to form building blocks like amino acids and nucleotides, which could have accumulated in water bodies making a "Primordial soup".

These building blocks could have combined and formed larger and more complex molecules like proteins and nucleic acids. These polymers then could assemble into small structures which made them capable of sustaining and replicating themselves and making more micro molecules like them. Oparin thought these might have been colonies of protein clustered together to carry out metabolism, While Haldane suggested that these macromolecules became enclosed in membranes to make cell-like structures.

But the basic idea of a stepwise, spontaneous formation of simple, then more complex, then self-sustaining biological molecules or assemblies is still at the core of most organized hypotheses to date. So, two more scientists tested Oparin and

Haldane's ideas they were Stanley Miller and Harold Urey. They experimented with Oparin and Haldane's idea in 1953 and found that organic molecules could be spontaneously produced under reducing conditions thought to resemble those of early Earth. After letting their experiment take a run of the week they found various types of amino acids, sugars, and other organic molecules but no large or complex molecules were found yet their experiment showed that at least some of the building blocks for these molecules could be formed spontaneously from simple compounds.

From the experiment carried out by Urey and Miller to try the idea of Oparin and Haldane, it seems reasonable to imagine that at least some organic structures could be formed abiotically on early Earth. How is the open question still?

Basis of Particle Physics

The Building of Particles: The world is made up of many millions of particles and substances. Each comprises different fundamentals and also different energies they got from their birth. The particles are too complicated to understand and researchers are doing their max to understand this fundamental thing.

The basics of particle physics generally deal with the two solid and fundamentally existing particles that are followed everywhere in our known universe. They are fermions and bosons.

This article made all the solid and smaller things together they make our universe. Fermions can interact with each other with negligible energy sources. While the boson makes all the stuff we see in the surrounding. The perfect example of a fermion and a boson are electrons and protons. Just as negative and positive, this example is a form of our well-known surroundings.

Particle physics teaches us how the particles in our universe work together and interact with each other in the ground state and also while transferring energy.

We have now started knowing the particles from close using the particle accelerator, which also gives us information about the nature and inner structure of the particle. Particle physics is also called High Energy Physics. All the particles that are present in our surroundings are generally made up of matter and radiation.

The standard model theory also explains the particles along with their energies and their existences and how they work on basis of calculations. It also promotes the theory of finding the newest and the oldest particle, that is Hibbs boson, and the gravitational field.

Particle table is also divided into a certain category, they are divided on basis of nature and their size and also the bonding they will make after having a collision with the same one. Protons and neutrons are made up of small particles called baryons which are usually made up of quarks. Some are produced by the process of scattering which also involves radioactive material. Those are called protons and neutrons. Some of the particles possess the property of wave-particle duality, this is generally a term in quantum mechanics which we will be learning in the coming chapter.

Wave-particle duality means a substance is also a particle or a wave depending on the nature and quantum environment. Similarly any fundamental can be a wave or a particle depending on the quantum state.

Some of the particles are also present in Hilbert space depending on their quantum state and their nature. Only those particles are present whose who are not composed of any other matter as a whole. Hilbert space is considered a vector space that is aligned by the quantum borders. Which has an inner product operation which allows the definition of a distance function. The cosmic microwave background is somehow responsible for the development of nature of the particle physics. All the observations that are made up to date and explained can be considered as the standard model of particle physics. The standard is thus generated from the continuous observations of the particles. The standard model also explains the nature of the quarks, which are smaller than atoms.

Quarks show unique behavior in their states which is upstate and downstate. There are 100s of particles and their variants discovered since the 1960s. Coming to the standard model all the diversities that a particle shows are proved by performing certain experiments on the particles. This is called the standard model which is technically more advanced and gives us all the proofs. Some experiments show deviations in the standard model such neutrinos mass experiment. As the standard model describes neutrinos as massless particles, this is the point we get some deviation.

History of particle physics:

The basic idea that all matter is made up of fundamental particles was put forth in the 6th century BC. This idea regained its boost in the 19th century when John Dalton was working on stoichiometry and found that each element that is present in the environment was made up of small unique and unknown particles. Then atom was discovered which was the smallest ever discovered. But just after that scientists discover that inside an atom there are electrons, neutrons, and protons present to give the atom enough balance to sustain its stability. Later in the 20th-century experiments on nuclear physics and quantum physics gave us the proof of nuclear fission in 1939 by Lise Meitner and also nuclear fusion by Hans Bethe.

This discovery gave rise to the development of nuclear weapons. As scientists have studied all the chemical reactions that were needed to make a nuclear bomb. Throughout 5 to 10 years after the revolution in particle physics different new particles were discovered by different scientists, which were experimentally and theoretically proved.

Some of the theories also need mathematical proof to support them. After the standard model was accepted all over the world all the fundamental particles were framed in the quantum field and also it created certain networks in the particles which were present in outer space. This gave rise to modern particle physics. The particle collider has contributed to finding several different particles and have changed the nature of particles which helped scientists to study standard model more. One of the most important theories among these is the

String theory, string theory explains the connection between the Quantum field and general relativity.

The particle accelerator also found different types of subatomic particles, which gave strong support to forming a standard model. They discovered that up quark and down quark is present in proton and neutron, while strange, bottom, up, and charm are heavy than others and can construct a whole particle.

They're also a second category which is leptons, which are of six types. Which 3 that are negatively charged are electron, muon, and tau and the other three are neutral in charge which means there is no charge. All of these subatomic particles need a charge to form a connection or a bond that is provided by the charges in the universe. They are the four forces. Taking the first force is the gravitational force, which is too weak to understand at by quantum level. Thus the subatomic particles are not affected by this or are negligible. The second is the electromagnetic force, which contains both electricity and magnetism. This force helps the electron to have a bond with the nucleus and be in the right orbit. The third is the strong nuclear force which helps subatomic particles to form a bond between protons and atomic nuclei. And the fourth last force is a weak nuclear force which allows the conversion of protons into neutrons in atomic nuclei.

The main reason the particle accelerator could not detect complex subatomic particles is the gravitational force because it's too weak. And it is also considered a mysterious force at a very basic level of quantum mechanics. As we don't have any traces of physical proof. Which is a reason it is not listed in the standard model.

Now lets us see the basic structure of the standard model of particle physics. As we know there are six types of quarks in the standard model and similarly, we have six subatomic particles which we called leptons of which three of them are electronically charged. But there is a subatomic particle called Hibbs Boson which is not completely explained or which is a mysterious particle to us.

Applications of Particle Physics:

Medical Sciences (Cancer Therapy)

Every highly advanced hospital uses this Cancer Therapy with the help of a Particle accelerator that produces X-Rays. Protons and Neutrons are also produced in the particle accelerator. The main purpose of the particle accelerator in medical science is to produce heavy ions for the treatment of diagnosis. There is nearly 6500 center hatch use this technology to overcome Cancer which have more than 2 crore people all around the world.

Industries:

While the industry is running it requires a high supply of electricity throughout the day. This is only possible because of cables which are made up of different materials. Thus, industries use superconducting material for making the cables rather than conventional material for fast electric supply and carrying maximum electricity. Particle physics will give a boost in this sector and advanced cables will be launched with the help of particle physics.

Biomedicines and Drug making:

Scientists use particle physics for studying the inner structure of proteins and many more, this helps scientists to study different biological processes which could also heal many diseases.

Computing:

The first all-world network is the world wide web created with the help of particle physics. It helped people communicate with each other very easily and efficiently. It also

organized different sessions and conferences with the help of
this technology.

Quantum Mechanics

Quantum mechanics is a branch of science that deals with the zoomed state of any matter that is present in the universe. This is very interesting and one of the most difficult, complex, and mysterious studies.

Quantum mechanics studies all the fundamentals of physics at a very basic quantum level. It also studies the subatomic particles easily. QM generally produces equations and predictions of the smallest particles and put forth their nature and work in front of us. QM can go up to quarks which are considered the smallest known matter. We can learn the states of the quark particles by applying quantum mechanics and its laws to matter. QM works on the principle of understanding the universe much better.

QM is also recognized as quantum physics as it includes equations and mathematical calculations just like physics. Classical laws of physics are different from quantum physics. Some of the classical physics laws failed at a very basic quantum level. Understanding quantum mechanics is a little more complex than our classical physics because it has its own set of rules and laws to follow. Quantum mechanics also explains the concept of matter and antimatter to the world.

Anti mater is somewhat the opposite of matter which works opposite and also has an opposite electric charge. It always keeps a track of the nature of waves and particles and the state of their existence. Neil Bohr and Max Plank are the fathers of quantum mechanics as they both first studied QM and introduced this to the world. QM makes you deal with the matter in our surroundings at a very small statue of atoms and subatomic particles.

QM is considered the starting point for many other terms such as quantum gravity, quantum theory, quantum field theory, quantum chemistry, and also quantum information. All the happenings and matter present in the universe are identical in their ways and classical physics explains those concepts at a very basic scale while quantum mechanics explains it more deeply and at a zoomed level. Most of the discoveries in classical physics take suppose of QM for their proof. Differs a lot from classical physics in terms of energy, atomic energy, and angular momentum. QM is used to prove some of the complex systems of the working of the universe. And all the predictions that were made on quantum mechanics were experimentally proved to be correct later.

QM does not make predictions on the states of matter or antimatter because the universe works on the factor of uncertainty, nothing in our universe is certain and remains the same all the time. It only gives us the possibilities and different ways to look after a certain phenomenon. To add more accuracy to the predictions of the QM, the concept of probability amplitude is used. It is a mathematical term in which probability is ensured by taking the square of the absolute value to a complex number. This is also called as Born rule.

For example, consider a waveform that is in an uncertain position in the universe and no one knows the exact position of the wave or a particle then by its last position and by applying the rule we can predict the position of the wave function. Even if, we don't predict the exact position of the particle or a wave exactly we can surely predict the position by some mathematical equations. We can't know the right position of a particle in space.

QM says that all the stuff that is present in the surrounding is in the form of waves, and suppose an observer is introduced at the same time the wave function collapse, and then we can see things in solid and physical form. Unless and until an observer is present all the surrounding things are in the waveform. Our brain is not capable of seeing the waves, thus when we see buildings and different structures, our brain converts them into physical and solid forms. Or else the buildings and structures are in the waveform unless we see them. This is a very weird science of quantum mechanics that has been proved. Quantum mechanics came into the picture just after classical physics couldn't explain some of the theories and all the fundamentals, there was a need for some different type of study to look after those failures. In the 1900s Max Plank gave a solution for the black body radiation problem with the help of quantum physics, and this was the decade when QM was introduced to the world.

Now we will see some of the interesting theories and factors of quantum mechanics which created curiosity among the people to gain more knowledge about QM.

The very first is quantum entanglement. We see quantum entanglement between two atoms or particles of the same substance, in which the two atoms or particles are entangled (are connected) even if the distance between them is infinite. And information transfer between is faster than the speed of light. This means when we point to the quark state of atom A if it is in upstate then the particle B will be in the down state. This information transfer between the two particles was carried out at a speed that is more than the speed of light. This type of factor is also called quantum pseudo-telepathy.

Quantum tunneling is also a weird phenomenon put forth by quantum mechanics. It is said that a particle that can go against its potential barrier can easily cross it, even if its kinetic energy is smaller than its initial or actual one. Talking about classical physics this experiment would have failed because our classical laws are different from quantum laws. In quantum mechanics, a wave can be a particle at the same time. This means at the same time it can take two different forms that are a wave and a particle.

First, we have to understand what is the difference between a wave and a particle. Consider a grain of sand a particle that has its kinetic energy as we squeezed the grain, we can impart a force to our hand which means it's solid and has a physical state which we can sense. While the waves are not solid as compared to particles. There are different possibilities in our universe which are related to quantum mechanics.

One of the interesting hypothetical theories is of multiverses, can our every action would create a different universe full of different possibilities and time sheets? This is very weird that each action is being considered and a new probability is posed by them. We can also sometimes experience some things that we think we have experienced before scientist suggest that these, experiences are a quick image of yourself living in an alternate universe. Just as a particle is present in all its possible states unless and until we see them.

Now we are going to see one of the most important and interesting experiments of quantum mechanics. This tells us how important an observer is in QM. Now one of the most appreciated experiments is the Delayed choice quantum eraser experiment, which tells us the dual nature of the particle. This famous experiment was performed to know the consequences of the double slit experiment of quantum mechanics and also the consequences of quantum entanglement. The delayed choice quantum eraser experiment shows the uneven paradox. Suppose a photon is thrown through the slit by a single path to the detector then it should enter the double slit as a particle for sure. And suppose the photon had come from two undefined paths then it must enter the double slit as a wave. If the whole experiment is reversed, while the photon is traveling then the photon should change its original state as it should be a wave or a particle. At the end of the experiment, a photon can change its decision depending on the external factor. That is an observer. In other, words this could be explained as when the observer is introduced at the end part of the experiment then he will observe it as a particle, just because we are not capable of observing the waves. And suppose we introduced the observer after the photon had traveled through the double slit it is sure that he should see a wave. But here is the main climax, even the observer is introduced after the double slit we see a particle. That means the photon had time traveled and passed the double slit as a particle. This whole experiment was performed several times and the results were shocking no wave had been seen when the observer is introduced.

Now lets us see how we use quantum physics in everyday life without even knowing. They can be very basic applications of our life and the factors are very fascinating. The most common application we see in day-to-day life is a computer which can be also called a quantum computer. If we look at, the basic parts of a computer, they are transistors very little part of all electronic stuff. All the things that small parts of a computer can do are switch a billion times in a minute. A transistor uses silicon as a primary element which is also a semiconductor. Semiconductors are also considered as the energy states which change along the condition provided to the transistor and this is where on-off switches are produced inside an electronic component. One can also add phosphor in this tech to increase or decrease the energy states of the material. All this minute technology relies on the quantum world.

Secondly, all the screens and cameras that we are using are working on the principle of semiconductors of the quantum world. Quantum mechanics is gaining more advancement and reaching a high technological height. Even this branch of physics is just 100 years old.

Next are the microprocessors. This is one of the most advanced electronic chips. We see this kind of chip in mobile phones laptops and so on. It can have a million transistors in it. All this is possible because of the advancement in quantum mechanics. Microprocessors carry our commands to the computer. Different types of video games are used to give you a better experience. Examples of microprocessors are intel, Ryzen, and Qualcomm.

Now one of the fascinating, applications of quantum mechanics is the Quantum computer. This one of the most powerful computers ever made in human history works on the principle of quantum mechanics.

When quantum mechanics was first developed, it was applied to models whose limit communication was that of unrelated ancient mechanics. For example, the well-known model quantum harmonic oscillator uses an unrelated expression of the kinetic power of the oscillator and thus is a quantum version of the classical harmonic oscillator. The problem arose with complex systems, which do not have good quantum numbers, and quantum chaos learns the relationship between ancient meanings and values in these systems.

Quantum decoherence is a method by which quantum systems lose coherence, and thus can show many common quantum effects: quantum superpositions become a possible mixture, and quantum binding becomes just a common correlation. Quantum coherence is usually not seen on a very large scale, except where temperatures are close to the perfect egg where quantum behavior may be most noticeable.

Many macroscopic structures of the classical system are a direct result of the quantum behavior of its components. For example, the stability of a mass (consisting of atoms and molecules that could quickly collapse under a single electric current), the solidity of solids, and the mechanical, thermal, chemical, physical, and magnetic properties are all the result of the interaction of an object. electrical charges under the rules of quantum mechanics.

Even though your guesses of both quantum theory and general relativity have been supported by strong and repetitive evidence, their incomprehensible processes are contradictory and prove very difficult to incorporate into a single, coherent, coherent model. Gravity is not important in many areas of particle physics, so integration between standard relation and quantum mechanics is not an urgent problem for those specific applications.

However, the lack of a proper theory of quantum gravity is a significant problem in visual cosmology and the search for the best physics specialist "Theory of Everything" (TOE). As a result, resolving the conflict between the two ideas became a major goal of physics in the 20th and 21st centuries. This TOE not only incorporates subatomic physics models but also acquires four basic natural forces in one force or a single object. Another suggestion to do so is string theory, which states that particles such as in point particle physics are replaced by one-sided objects called strings. Rope theory explains how these strings spread across space and interact with each other.

On larger scales larger than the cord scale, the character unit looks like a normal particle, with its size, charge, and other factors determined by the vibration of the cord. In the theory of ropes, one of the most common types of rope vibrations is associated with graviton, a quantum mechanical particle that holds gravity.

Another result of the mathematical laws of quantum mechanics is the phenomenon of quantum interference, which is often demonstrated by double-slit testing. In the basic version of this test, a compatible light source, similar to a laser beam, illuminates a perforated plate with two matching slits, and the light passing through them is reflected on the screen behind the plate.

The nature of the light wave causes light waves passing through both squares to disrupt, producing light and black bands on the screen - an effect that would not be expected if the light was combined with ancient particles. However, light is always available to be placed on the screen in different places, such as individual particles rather than waves; the disturbance pattern arises from the various densities of these particles on the screen.

In addition, experimental versions that include icons on slits find that each photon found passes through one location (as would be the ancient particles), and not both holes (as it would a wave). However, such experiments indicate that particles do not form a disruptive pattern when one discovers what they are going through. Other atomic scale trades, such as electrons, are found to show similar behavior when fired at a double square. This behavior is known as wave-particle duality.

When quantum systems interact, the result can be the creation of quantum entanglement: their structures are so interdependent that the meaning of all of them only in individual parts is no longer available. Erwin Schrödinger called entanglement " a characteristic feature of quantum mechanics, which compels its exit from the ancient lines of thought". Quantum entanglement empowers the opposing features of quantum pseudo-telepathy and can be an important aid in communication agreements, such as the distribution of quantum keys and large-scale coding.

Contrary to popular belief, the catch does not allow sending signals faster than light, as evidenced by the theory of the absence of communication. Another possible open-ended experiment is the "hidden variables", hypothetical structures that are more important than the quantities referred to in quantum theory itself, information that can allow for more accurate predictions than quantum theory. The set of results, most importantly Bell's theory, has shown that the broad categories of such hidden flexible concepts are incompatible with quantum physics. In Bell's view, if the environment works by any of the hidden environmental variables theory, Bell's test results will be restricted in a certain, measurable way.

Many Bell experiments have been performed, using coherent particles, and showing results that do not conform to the limits set by hidden location variables.

The rules of quantum mechanics assert that the regional area of the system is Hilbert's space and that the system detects Hermitian operators working on vectors in that space - although they do not tell us what Hilbert's space or operators are. These can be appropriately selected to obtain a quantum definition of a quantum system, a step needed in making physical predictions. An important guide to making these decisions is the principle of communication, the heuristic one that states that the predictions of quantum mechanics are reduced to those of high-tech mechanics in the system of large quantum numbers. One can also start at the old standard model of a particular system, and then try to guess the basic quantum model that can produce the old model at the end of the connection. This method is known as quantization.

Albert Einstein, also one of the founders of quantum theory, was concerned about its apparent failure to respect known metaphysical principles, such as determinism and space. Einstein's long discussions with Bohr about the meaning and nature of quantum mechanics are now known as Bohr-Einstein debates. Einstein believed that basic quantum mechanics should be a theory that explicitly forbids distant action. He asserted that quantum mechanics were incomplete, a theory that was formal but not fundamental, such as the way thermodynamics works, but that the basic theory behind it was mathematical mechanics.

In 1935, Einstein and his collaborators Boris Podolsky and Nathan Rosen published an argument that the local system suggested the limitations of quantum mechanics, a theory of thought later called the Einstein-Podolsky-Rosen paradox. In 1964, John Bell pointed out that local EPR goal, as well as determinism, was incompatible with quantum mechanics: they suggested barriers to the relationships produced by distinct systems, now known as Bell's inequalities, which could be broken by adjoining particles.

Since then several experiments have been performed to determine this relationship, with the result that it actually violates Bell's inequality, and thus falsifies local integration and determination.

In the early 19th century, chemical experiments by John Dalton and Amedeo Avogadro reinforced the atomic theory of the story, a theory that James Clerk Maxwell, Ludwig Boltzmann, and others built on to develop a kinetic gas theory. The success of kinetic theory provided further confidence in the notion that matter is made up of atoms, yet this theory had flaws that could only be solved by the development of quantum mechanics. Although the earliest conception of atoms from Greek philosophy was that they were inseparable units - the word "atom" is derived from a Greek word meaning "indestructible" - the 19th century saw the formation of ideas about the subatomic structure.

One of the most important discoveries in that regard was the discovery by Michael Faraday in 1838 of light caused by a breakdown of electricity inside a low-pressure glass tube. Julius Plücker, Johann Wilhelm Hittorf, and Eugen Goldstein carried on and developed Faraday's work, which led to the identification of cathode radiation, J.H.

Spin is also very important in quantum mechanics due to the discovery of quantum entanglement, which Einstein called "a spooky action far away." It is possible to create two electrons so that their circuits are not independent; when the spins of these electrons are measured, there is a strong (anti-) connection between the effects, even if the electrons are separated by a very large distance to influence each other! The fact that this relationship cannot be explained by other invisible variables hidden in the visible system is a theorem in quantum mechanics known as the Bell theorem. Capturing, quantum teleportation and the general deception of high-ranking regional circuits have major implications for encryption and are the basis for the emerging field of quantum computing.

Dark Energy

Dark energy is one of the fascinating and mysterious forms of energy in our universe. About which we know nothing as compared to its significance. In terms of cosmology dark energy is considered an unknown form of energy that affects space-time on a very large scale.

Even though we are knowing very little about dark energy scientists know that dark energy is somewhat present in each aspect of space. Scientists even couldn't find the source of the dark energy but they know that dark energy exists in many forms that affect the cosmos. Dark energy is still mysterious even after considering all its known factors.

Dark energy is considered a hypothetical form of energy just because physically we have not detected its presence. But surely many cosmological bodies are affected by it. It also shows variations and fluctuations in terms of quantum. Hypothetically dark energy can also be called gravity, but the parameters can be very different. Nature and the physical state can be different. Some of the theories suggest that dark energy is responsible for the expansion of the universe, which might be true but is yet to be true. Many scientists think that this might be a possibility.

Now coming to the nature and energy of dark energy. Dark energy exerts negative energy tools surrounding space and celestial bodies. In our observable universe, there is about 72% of dark energy, among the total energy density of our universe. Dark energy also accelerates the rate of expansion of our universe over time. This means the expansion of the universe is not in a constant state it changes over time.

Dark energy is the opposite of gravity it releases energy and pressure but in the opposite direction to that of gravity. Though it occupies over 72% of our universe we just have a basic idea of it and its working. In the future, the releasing power of dark energy will increase so much that the acceleration of expanding universe will go beyond its limit tearing all the galaxies and space-time also the celestial bodies. It can also tear the fabrics of space and time including subatomic particles. This is called Big Rip. As the beginning of the universe is considered a Big Bang, the end of the universe is considered a Big Rip. Dark energy is somewhat the same as negative matter or negative energy.

It also deals with quantum fluctuations and the positive matter and negative energy within the cosmos. Considering one scenario of dark energy we will take an example that came in front of scientists, and they were not able to explain so they named that scenario d energy.

They discovered a star, which was more luminous than our star, and two planets were seen orbiting the star but the thing was the orbiting speed of the planets was more than its limit, scientists made calculations that with this orbiting speed the planets should not remain in the orbit of the star but they were shocked after the results were displayed. The two planets were orbiting this star at a high amount of speed without getting off the orbit. Scientists named that unknown force that was holding the two planets dark energy, just because they were unable to explain the physics behind that stuff. Dark energy has attracted many scientists towards it but very few got succeeded in knowing the actual physics and working behind dark energy. In our universe, many energies are stronger than gravity. Some of them have stronger repulsive forces such as dark energy. The negative and repulsive force of dark energy is more than the repulsive force of gravity. This force is way more to push all the matter away from each other like galaxies and other celestial bodies. Thus, dark energy is considered antigravity in many aspects of the universe.

Drawing our attention to such mysterious objects and energies makes the universe more interesting to understand and makes different types of theories. Space is all about unexplored things that meet new challenges in our life to explore more.

Before knowing the current condition, we must know the beginning of our universe. How it started and how it will end in the future. For this, we have to know the general evolution of the universe. Thus, we can take the reference of the cosmic microwave background to establish a connection between dark energy and evolution. How dark energy can affect evolution? Can energy cause the fluctuations between unknown forces of the universe? Well yes, this all can take place if we considered things hypothetically. The universe can understand adequately to achieve great scientific development in space technology. There, are much cosmological research by which we can understand nature and all the fundamental properties of dark energy.

Dark energies can be of two types. Both terms are somewhat related to each other from the very beginning, let us consider they are related from the time they were produced. One of them is the cosmological constant. This can be represented by a constant amount of energy dispersed among all, filling all the empty spaces with this kind of constant energy. We can also say that dark energy is the constant amount of energy that is present in our universe. This kind of dynamic quantity of energies can vary from each other which can also vary from time to time.

There are also some scalar empty spaces in our universe that can be filled with this kind of constant energy as well. All empty spaces can be considered as zero-point radiation of the universe, which is called vacuum energies, this is the second type of dark energy. Thus, all the scalar spaces of energy and the cosmological constants are very hard to distinguish. They both can have the same amount of energy and nature is almost the same. Because of the toy model of the nature of cosmology, scientists believe that an accurate relativistic structure of our universe based on all the scales of the real universe can differ because of dark energy.

The cosmological constant we saw can exhibit any type of energy that is positive or negative. In this, constant energy can be zero, and hence it is called vacuum energy. The cosmological constant was put forth by Albert Einstein to have mathematical and theoretical proof of the gravitational field equation. Which would also give proof of the Static energy of our universe. Einstein took the factor of dark energy to prove the balance of gravity. The symbol for the cosmological constant was capital Lambda, it was stated that the cosmological constant required space or vacuum energy to roll the gravity as a negative mass that is spread in interstellar space.

Later, the example of fine-tuning was in front of all the scientists they realized that the static Universe cannot be able to have a balance between dark energy and gravity. The given fundamental is completely unstable if the Universe expands even slightly more the expansion will release all the types of dark energy and the vacuum energy which was stored in terms of the blank spaces. Considering this equation the universe will contract more in terms of expansion, and we'll show on usual happening.

Thus, such disturbances are responsible for the distribution of matter throughout the universe. In 1929 Edwin Hubble proved that the universe is expanding and it is not static at all. This was one of the finest discoveries in terms of cosmology.

Now we will discuss what inflationary dark energy is. In 1980 professor Alan Guth proposed that negative energy or negative pressure that can be similar in terms of dark energy could have cosmic inflation at the time of The Big Bang. Inflation is considered the repulsive force that is similar to the dark energy which is responsible for the expansion of the universe slightly after the Big Bang, this proved that the cosmic microwave background was in existence at the time of the Big Bang. Scientists believe that inflationary dark energy could occur at places where the energy density is larger than the dark energy. This type of inflationary dark energy would have been completely ended when the universe was only a fraction of a second old.

These were the standard models for the inflationary dark energy that has been accepted all over the world and by all the scientists which means the cosmological constant that was discovered by Albert Einstein is considered to be irrelevant to the universe. All these, models predict only one thing the energy present in the total Universe which is considered the energy density can be similar to the critical density or can be equal to it.

All this, standard models of inflationary dark energy were found to be true after Alan Guth proposed his theories on dark energy. These energy theories also gave proof for the formation of clusters and newly active galaxies. Later on, discovered that they need a value which is lower than the Hubble constant to prove the observations. These large differences between gravity and inflationary dark energies which we might call dark energy. which we know nothing about.

Scientists required high measurements and observations to determine the expansion rate of the universe over time. The expansion rate of the universe is not constant it changes over time to time, they have to carry on certain experiments to know the current rate of expansion of the universe. In general relativity, it is explained that the expansion rate can be acquired from the curvature of the universe and a well-known cosmological equation state. This fundamental factor can be explained by the relationship between the matter, energy, pressure, vacuum, and energy density of a region of interstellar space. Measuring the equation of dark energy is still a challenge to many scientists.

The nature of dark energy is more mysterious than that of dark matter. Dark energy is considered energy that is not as dense as dark matter. It cannot interact directly with celestial objects and energy density but it will interact directly with gravity. The very first reason that dark energy affects gravity is its amount of presence which is 68%. Even though dark Energy is very thin it can occupy all the empty spaces of space and time very easily.

One of the supporting, theories that we don't know about dark energy is that energy does not reflect with the sunlight and the mass is almost negligible. And even with the most powerful telescope, we couldn't see the existence of dark energy and dark matter.

In all the empty spaces of our interstellar universe and space there exist dark energy which gave rise to the different nature and fundamentals of the universe and its energy densities. Dark energy can also have more energy densities than any other force in our universe. The, more empty spaces in the universe the amount of dark energy present in empty spaces makes our universe expand. We have to put this extra gravity known as the dark energy to know the working and fundamentals of a universe and even in the simulations we have to put this dark energy to know beyond space. We have to bring cosmic microwave background into consideration to know the existence of dark energy because cosmic microwave background was present at the time of the Big Bang. Due to this cosmic microwave background, scientists came to know the tentative age of the universe which is 13.77 billion years old, and that atoms make up only 4.6 % of that universe.

Particle physicists came to know that there is something that doesn't interact with us and even with light particles and also with telescopes these particles are somewhat very small and is present at the quantum level that had been affected by gravity itself and their performing their tasks. Dark energy is invisible but it Can attract our matter into it, showing unusual happenings.

Dark energy can be used in many terms as dark energy is the opposite of gravity in this energy accelerates the universe's expansion rate and we can have information about large-scale structures. Similarly, this type of technique is used to measure the expansion rate of the universe by knowing the luminosity rate of the stars that are distant from our Galaxy. supernovas are an example of largescale objects by which the expansion rate is measured. In some hypothetical theories, it is also possible to use the dark energy of first space as a power source but we cannot completely rely on that theory. As dark energy is not detectable very easily it is very hard for us to liberate that energy for our well-being. There is a theory for dark energy is responsible for the expansion of our universe, which is called Phantom dark energy, proving that not only the expansion is accelerating but also the acceleration increasing over time.

There, are certain proof for dark energy which includes three independent factors that are known as distance measurement and their relation to the redshift. which supports the theory of the expansion of the universe and proves that Universe has expanded more in the latter of his life this is just because the expansion trade or the acceleration is increasing over time.   need a strong negative pressure to explain the factors of observation of acceleration of the expansion of the universe.

According to Albert Einstein's theory of relativity, it will need a high pressure of a substance to its gravitational attraction to identify heavy mass objects. In different types of theory, it is suggested that a higher amount of negative pressure is required to sustain constant acceleration.

No kind of force or energy can stop the acceleration of the universe against dark energy. The universe could not have specific flexibility to all this, small forces to act against dark energy. Dark energy can be considered as the total amount of energy in the universe which is separated by its geometry to sustain a balance between the energies and space-time.

All types of models of inflation tell that the density of the Cosmos can be very close to the critical density. In 1985 different type of cosmological research was based on the critical density of the energy which was spread in all parts of the universe. According to their observations, there is 95% of the cold dark matter and 5% of the usual ordinary matter later, models were found to be true, forming different types of galaxies and clusters that require dark matter to form. It was observed that the Hubble constant was decreasing than predicted by observing distant galaxies and their formation calculation. Higher accuracy measurements for the expansion of the universe are needed to understand how the expansion rate changes over time. In general, the emergence of the expansion rate is estimated from the cosmic curve and the cosmological equation of the state (the relationship between temperature, pressure, composite properties, strength, and vacuum density in any space region). Measuring the equation of the dark energy state is one of the great efforts in observational cosmology today. In addition to its true nature, dark energy may need to have strong negative pressure to explain the apparent acceleration of the expansion of the universe.

According to the general relation, the internal pressure of an object influences its attraction to other objects as it does its density. This is because the apparent amount that causes objects to produce gravitational effects is the stress-energy tensor, which contains both the force (or matter) of the object and its pressure.

In normal cosmology, there are three parts of the universe: matter, rays, and dark forces. A matter is anything whose density is measured by the opposite cube of a scale element, i.e., $\rho \propto a - 3$, whereas radiation is anything that measures the negative force of the fourth-dimension element ($\rho \propto a - 4$). This can be accurately understood: with normal particles in a cube-shaped box, doubling the edge of the box reduces congestion (and hence the density of energy) by eight elements. In radiation, the decrease in energy density is great, because increasing local distance also causes redness.

Some people argue that the only indicators of the presence of dark energy are the perception of distance measurements and related redshifts. The posterior anisotropies of the cosmic microwave and the baryon acoustic oscillations only help to indicate that the distances to the given red space are larger than might be expected.

Supernovae are useful in cosmology because they are the best-quality candles in all cosmological stages. They allow researchers to measure the elasticity of the universe by looking at the relationship between the distance of the object and its redness, which gives it a step backward for us. Relationships are almost equal, according to Hubble's law. It is easy to measure a redshift, but finding the distance of the object is very difficult. Often, astronomers use ordinary candles: objects for internal light or full size.

The presence of dark forces, in any form, is necessary to combine the measured geometry of space with the total number of objects in space. Estimates of cosmic microwave background (CMB) anisotropies indicate that the universe is near the surface. For the universe to be flat, the density of the atmosphere must be equal to the critical density.

The total amount of matter in the universe (including biomass and black matter), as measured by the CMB spectrum, accounts for about 30% of the critical density. This means that there is an additional source of energy that will count for the remaining 70%. The seven-year Wilkinson Microwave

Anisotropy Probe (WMAP) spacecraft estimates that the universe is made up of 72.8% black matter, 22.7% black matter, and 4.5% normal. The work done in 2013 based on CMB's Planck spacecraft observations provided a more accurate estimate of black energy of 68.3%, 26.8% black matter, and 4.9% normal. The study of the effect of dark energy on a large structure involves measuring the subtle distortions in the formation of galaxies resulting from the bending of space with intervening elements, a phenomenon known as "weak lensing." Sometime in the last few billion years, black energy became dominant in the universe and thus prevented more galaxies and galaxy clusters from forming. This change in the structure of the universe is revealed by weak lenses.

Another measure is found in calculating the total number of galaxies in the universe to measure the size of the universe and the extent to which that volume is growing.

It is distributed evenly throughout the universe, not only in space but also in time - in other words, its effect is not dissolved as the universe grows. Equal distribution means that dark energy has no local gravity, but has a global impact on the universe. This leads to abhorrent forces, which often accelerate the expansion of the universe. Its rate of expansion and acceleration can be measured based on Hubble's law. These estimates, along with other scientific data, have confirmed the existence of dark forces and provide an estimate of how much mysterious matter exists.

As the galaxy approaches the horizon, the light emanating from it will change dramatically red, until the wavelength is too great to be seen in action and the galaxies appear to be disappearing. The Planet Earth, the Milky Way, and the Milky Way galaxy of which it is a part would all remain intact as the entire universe recedes and disappears from view. In this case, the Local Group will eventually die of heat, just as was thought of in the flat, controlled atmosphere before measuring cosmic acceleration.

There are some additional theories about the future of the universe. The phantom power model of the black energy results in a different increase, which does not mean that the active black energy continues to grow until it overcomes all other forces in the universe. Under this scenario, dark energy could eventually penetrate all the structures of gravity, including galaxies and solar systems, and eventually conquer the electromagnetic field to separate the atoms themselves, destroying the universe by "massive fragmentation". On the other hand, dark energy may fade with time or be appealing. Such uncertainty exposes the potential for gravity to exist and lead the universe to allow itself to enter by "Big Crunch", or possibly to have a dark energy cycle, meaning a replica of the space cycle that always multiplies (Big Explosion and ends up being I). -Big Crunch) lasts approximately 312 years. Although none of this is supported by surveillance, it is not excluded.

Guessing the future can be very different from different models of dark energy. According to cosmological, any other model predicts that acceleration will continue indefinitely, the result will be that galaxies outside the Local Group will have a linear speed that progresses over time, eventually exceeding light speed.

This is not a special violation of the relationship because the concept of "speed" used here differs from that of speed in a local reference framework, which is still restricted to light speed in any large object (see Using the appropriate range of subtitle dialogue to describe any cosmology-related speed theory). A study published in 2020 questioned the validity of the important assumption that light in the supernovae does not differ from star age, and suggests that dark energy may not exist. Leading researcher of the new study, Young-Wook Lee of Yonsei University, said: "Our results show that dark energy from SN cosmology, which led to the 2011 Nobel Prize in Physics, maybe the artifact of weak and untrue assumptions."

Many of the problems with this paper were raised by other cosmologists, including Adam Riess, who won the 2011 Nobel Prize for dark supremacy.

Dark Matter

Dark matter is one of the mysterious forms of matter just like dark energy. We cannot see the dark matter through telescopes. But we are having traces of it. It is considered a hypothetical form of matter which scientist think can interact with other celestial bodies. There are certain fields of energy spread throughout the universe one of them is an electromagnetic field, it is seen that dark matter does not interact with any energy fields.

There are many views and hypothetical theories suggested by different space scientists to explain the evolution of dark matter. Dark matter cannot emit reflect or any of the subatomic particles including photons gravitons or any kind of electromagnetic radiation in space. Dark matter comes with a very convincing point that it occupies most of the vacant space beyond the solar system.

Dark matter can affect celestial objects in many aspects without our even knowing by us. Just because we cannot trace dark matter, particularly in a specific region these are the challenges faced by scientists in the study of dark matter. It also affects the basic quantum level to a larger extent as we don't have the Technologies to have such micro measurements. It can also interact with highly charged particles that are formed at the time of the Big Bang.

Dark matter is considered to be 85% of the total universe. dark matter has its evolution and influence on the different celestial bodies and energy fields. It is really difficult for scientists to study dark matter as we cannot observe it, but still, scientists are finding out a solution to know exactly what is dark matter by using certain theories that can relate to the cosmological bodies and can give us micro measurements on the existence of that matter. Scientists suggested that dark matter is infinite and abundant in space only one thing is there, we are not getting traces of it. The working of the galaxies would have been different if the dark matter wouldn't show so its influence on these Galaxies.

Dark matter has affected the gravitational pull and the timesheet of certain galaxies to a greater extent. This can be a reason for the fluctuations of radio signals from distant galaxies. This is only the way to study the galaxies that are far away from us using their light and radio signals to calculate the distance from the Milky Way galaxy.

Cosmic microwave background promotes the theory of dark matter as it was present from the beginning of the big bang. This is very crucial evidence for scientists to know what dark matter is. Cosmic microwave background would show certain fluctuations in the wave graph introduced by the scientist These, fluctuations are indeed proof that dark matter has a certain impact on the celestial bodies and also at the micro level that we called as Quantum level.

The structure of the quantum-level state of the universe is very different from the classical state of Physics, thus gravitational lensing can be a factor along with cosmic microwave background to know the traces of dark matter. according to the theory of the expansion of the universe dark matter is continuously increasing at a very high rate the energy which is responsible for the expansion of the universe can be called dark energy and the area that is formed during the expansion is unknown to us can be called as dark matter. The universe is hard to explain with the classical laws of Physics we have to increase our measurements and formulas to have the measurements of subatomic particles too. This will help us to learn more about energy densities and hypothetical energies like dark matter and dark energy. Therefore, we have to apply the laws of quantum mechanics to study the zoomed state of our universe.

As no one has observed that matter till now it can interact with simple baryonic matter and radiation. Scientists think that it cannot interact simply with Gravity. As the dark matter is considered to be non-baryonic by scientists it can be made with subatomic particles. we are talking about the subatomic particles that are completely unknown to us, which are mysterious to us just because the definition of dark matter is not still introduced to us.

There are many experiments conducted to study dark matter and to observe dark matter but to date, no one has succeeded to have a trace of it. The main purpose was to study the particles that are present in the dark matter but none of the experiments succeeded. Many of the communities of scientists still believe that the existence of dark metal is true though they have measurements they cannot explain to the scientist with the help of classical physics law scientists are still finding new ways to study it.

Scientists have also proved that certain modifications are required in general relativity to prove the existence and physical proof of the dark matter. The Hunt for dark matter started in 1884. The first scientist to come up with the theory of the existence of dark matter was the astronomer Jacobus Kapteyn. It was the time when scientists realized that there was something beyond our universe space and time that they called dark celestial bodies.

Jan Oort put forth the theory of the existence of dark matter in 1932. He was studying the basic celestial bodies in our neighborhood and suddenly found the Super Galaxy plane that was later determined as dark matter because its measurements were too micro to capture. Talking about the observational shreds of evidence of dark matter, considering our Galaxy Milky Way arms of all characters see around the Galaxy center of the universe. city of the spiral arms of the Milky Way galaxy decreases while reseeding velocity decreases. Considering the luminosity of the galaxies we can determine the exact position and velocity of the Galaxy from the other celestial bodies which can give us direct proof of some mysterious forms of energies and matter acting on the celestial bodies beyond our reach.

There is a great sign of dark matter in the evolution of the universe since the big bang. Great questions were raised in the 21st century regarding what exactly is dark matter, after which different scientists came up with certain explanations and hypothetical theories which gave us the basic idea of what dark is. Now the nature of direct matter is completely unknown and mysterious to us. We have to know the major components of the universe that were created at the time of the Big bang and to understand what dark matter i, basic level information.

Most of the convincing hypothetical theories suggest that it is made of the elementary particles that are created at the time of the big Bang which created our universe. The supporting theory for dark matter is the new particles that existed predicted by the hypothetical theories that don't obey the laws of the standard model of particle physics.

Only one particle cannot comprise the whole dark matter and could not provide us with every answer regarding it, for the key answer should be in deep cosmological aspects. We should also focus on the fundamental particles that approach the superposition wave which can also be called electromagnetic waves. One edition, known as cold dark matter tells us that the particles which are the opposite of the dark matter cannot move with the speed of light.

Dark matter can be detected by many observational methods by knowing the cosmological microwave background and the receding velocity and speed of stars and planets. Space is spread at an infinite level in all directions dividing the space timesheet into all the possible dimensions, so there are different types of clusters and local groups present in the observable universe which can help us get a trace of dark matter. Types of clusters, emit large amounts of X-rays in all possible directions near these high-mass celestial bodies. Different types of pieces of evidence are introduced in front of scientists for dark matter, there are different types of properties of dark matter which we can learn and exhibit are scientific experiments on it. One, of the difficult tasks, is to trace the location as the space-time sheet is dilated in all the possible directions and in all the possible dimensions in space it is hard for us to detect The Invisible matter and to know its physical properties.

There is one method by which we can know the exact location or the approximate location of direct matter which is gravitational lensing, it can help us in many ways in knowing the physical properties as the dark matter of higher mass distorts the light coming from the galaxies and stars and create a distance image in which is captured by our telescopes.

We have to perform this experiment on a large scale which means the larger amount of sky is visible to us hence it is easy for scientists to trace the pieces of evidence of dark matter using gravitational lensing. Detection of dark matter is only possible with the help of high mathematical calculations and appropriate detectors which can pass with the weak signals of the universe and can detect very rare matter, as dark matter, interact with the surrounding it is possible for us to detect the weak Signals and to get off the address of dark matter.

We can also distinguish the signal types of the universe ranging from low to higher because as dark matter has electromagnetic impulses that have a very low frequency. We have to detect it with a high amount, of appropriate calculations. the wave detector which we are using to detect the weak signals of dark matter should be kept behind a wall-like structure to prevent it from colliding with other Cosmic Rays or other energy densities. We have to distinguish this high amount of electromagnetic signal from the weak signal.

At the time of the Big Bang different types of frequency and microwave signals were produced just like cosmological microwave background it created different types of fluctuations in space and time which created cavities just as cracks in the space-time sheet by using this evidence we can know the appropriate location of finding the dark matter which might be in these cavities that are created at the time of big bang due to fluctuations. The universe is made up of different kinds of mysterious things that are still unknown to us, thus following curiosity and simultaneously achieving technological advancement is helping mankind to find answers to this question. there are different types of amplifiers available to amplify the frequency that is coming from millions of light years away from us.

One of the amplifiers is a superconducting quantum interference device which is also known aa s SQUID amplifier that will help us get what dark matter is.

Considering the vastness of the Universe it is spread at an infinite amount in all the possible directions there are certain frequencies or waves world as gamma rays or gravitons and different cosmological energies that can help us get the rest of dark matter and they can easily be detected in our amplifiers for a radio telescope, as dark matter also has some particles of antimatter present in it which help us persistence through a radio telescope. This kind of cosmological happening can take place in the center of the Galaxy which can produce a larger sum of fluctuations. The energy densities can directly affect the antimatter and different types of rays and also gravitons.

Here come the concept of dark matter and anti-dark matter which are different from each other we can just say they are opposite. Dark matter and anti-dark matter can produce when there are deviations in the gravitational fields of two celestial bodies, these deviations are enough to make a frequency wave that can be easily detectable by our radio telescopes. There are many hypothetical theories protective that dark matter has formed due to the collision of two subatomic particles that have an impact on the basic level of quantum mechanics. As it is a hypothetical theory different types of energy densities can act as particle accelerators to create high-frequency waves which cannot reflect we refract photons in any of the possible directions, this kind of frequencies and the place where they are present can be called dark matter.

It also has been suggested that the antimatter particles which deviate not the ordinary matter.

Large galaxy redshift surveys may be used to map a three-dimensional galaxy distribution. These maps are slightly distorted due to the estimated distances from the targeted redshifts; redshift contains a contribution from the so-called unique galaxy speed over Hubble's main expansion term. On average, large clusters grow slower than cosmic meanings due to gravity, while voids grow faster than average.

On a redshift map, the galaxies in front of a large cluster have radial velocities extending toward it and have red dots slightly higher than the mean distance, while the galaxies at the back of the larger cortex are slightly lower in their distance. This effect causes large clusters to appear squash on the radial side, and the voids are extended. Their angular positions are unaffected. This effect is not visible in any single building as the exact shape is unknown, but can be measured on a scale over many buildings.

It was predicted in bulk by Nick Kaiser in 1987 and was first measured in 2001 by the 2dF Galaxy Redshift Survey. The results are consistent with the Lambda-CDM model.

In 2015-2017, the idea that dense dark matter is formed by the original dark holes came back following the results of measurements of gravitational waves that found a combination of black holes in the center. Black holes with about 30 solar masses are not predicted to form by the fall of a star (usually less than 15 solar masses) or by the inclusion of black holes in galactic centers (millions or billions of solar mass). It was suggested that black holes with a medium density caused the fusion found formed in the first tropical atmosphere due to the collapse of dense areas.

A recent study of about a thousand supernovae found no cases of magnetic resonance lensing, in which about eight would be expected if the black holes in the middle — the mass exceeds a certain width account for the mass of dark matter.

The possibility that dark atom-sized black holes are an integral part of dark matter has been determined by measuring the positron and electron fluxes outside the solar heliosphere by the Voyager spacecraft Smaller black holes are said to emit Hawking rays. The fluxes obtained, however, were very low and did not have the expected energy spectrum, suggesting that small black holes were not wide enough to deal with dark matter. However, research and theories suggest that black-density dark media accounts continue from 2018, including ways to cool dark objects, and the question remains unknown.

By 2019, the lack of microlensing effects on Andromeda Vision suggests that small black holes do not exist. However, there is still a much smaller unrestricted range than can be limited by optical microlensing detection, where the original black holes may control all dark matter.

The possibility that dark atom-sized black holes are an integral part of dark matter has been determined by measuring the positron and electron fluxes outside the solar heliosphere by the Voyager spacecraft Smaller black holes are said to emit Hawking rays. The fluxes obtained, however, were very low and did not have the expected energy spectrum, suggesting that small black holes were not wide enough to deal with dark matter. However, research and theories suggest that black-density black media accounts continue from 2018, including ways to cool black objects, and the question remains unknown. In 2019, the lack of microlensing effects on Andromeda detection suggests that small black holes do not exist.

So far there has never been a well-established claim of dark matter detection from direct detection tests, leading to high solid weight limits and a cross-sectional interaction with the nuclei of such black particles. DAMA / NaI and the most recent DAMA / LIBRA experimental collaboration have identified annual fluctuations in the incidence of their finders, which they say is due to something dark. This results in the expectation that as the Earth orbits the Sun, the speed of the detector associated with a halo of dark matter will vary by a small amount. This claim has not been confirmed yet and conflicts with negative results from other tests such as LUX, Super CDMS, and XENON100. Because it is dark, the dark matter by definition does not emit, reflect, or refract any kind of light. Dark matter and normal matter are therefore separated as a result of the collision as the dark matter clumps from the two clusters move ahead of the hot gas (most of the normal matter). Around heavier objects, gravitational lensing bends light more noticeably. Such an impact would not exist if hot gas made up the majority of the clusters. Instead, these results demonstrate the need for dark matter, which we cannot see but which must have mass in order to have such a potent gravitational pull.

Quantum Gravity

Quantum gravity is somewhat the same as gravity and gravitational waves. It acts as a separate factor in terms of space and time. first of all, we will know what Quantum and gravity mean at a basic level. Considering the first world Quantum means small almost negligible matter that have a great impact on space-time and the universe and secondly Gravity here gravity means the amount of energy that each quark exhibit on the surrounding matter.

Thus, quantum gravity can be defined as the amount of energy of a quark applied to the surrounding matter, which acts as gravity and gravitational waves is called quantum gravity. Quantum gravity waves can have minute deviations and fluctuations on the differentiable matter of space and time. All the particles present in the universe irrespective of their size shape and mass can have a basic connection to quantum waves.

Quantum gravity is somewhat considered a hypothetical form of energy, just because of the lack of pieces of evidence and traces. It is difficult for scientists to trace and have a detailed observation of these waves.

There are different types of forces that are widely spread in our universe, which are directly explained by quantum mechanics. Just because the effects of the quantum factors rule the basic laws of physics. There is only one factor with which we can understand Gravity which is Einstein's general theory of relativity it is described in such a way that it explains classical physics along with space-time dilation. In the general theory of relativity, the nature of the black hole is perfectly explained with the help of space-time. It also creates a basic hypothesis of what's inside a Black hole which is explained by relativity.

We all need a Theory that is beyond the general relativity of Einstein to measure the space-time curvature which is at the center of the black hole. Gravity and gravitational wave come under classical physics while Quantum gravity comes under the subject of quantum mechanics which is very diverse. There is some set of rules for following classical physics as well as quantum physics because the level of consideration of the small matter is different between these two factors. Now we are going to see the basics of the Quantum Field and would try to understand the fundamentals of the quantum energies which we might describe as Quantum Gravity. as we go to the quantum level to study gravity all the deviations from the energy sources and fluctuations would result in different types of wave formation. This would lead us to the different sources of energy that can be spread out from a black hole.

Much of the difficulty in connecting these theories at all energy scales stems from the different assumptions they make about how the universe works. General relativity models gravity as the curvature of spacetime. John Archibald Wheeler's slogan state.

On the other hand, quantum field theory is usually formulated in the plane spacetime used in special relativity. No theory has yet proved successful in explaining the general situation in which quantum-mechanically model matter dynamics affect the curvature of spacetime. If we try to treat gravity simply as another quantum field, the resulting theory is not renormalizable. Even in the simple case where the curvature of spacetime is fixed a priori, the quantum field theory Development becomes more difficult mathematically, and many ideas that physicists use in flat spacetime in quantum field theory are no longer applicable.

Loop quantum gravity takes seriously the general relativity insight that space-time is a dynamic field and, therefore a quantum object. Their second idea is that the quantum discreteness that governs the particle-like behavior of other field theories (such as photons in electromagnetic fields) also influences the structure of space.   The main result of loop quantum gravity is the derivation of the granular structure of space at the Planck length. This is derived from the following considerations: In electromagnetism, the quantum operator representing the energy at each frequency of the field has a discrete spectrum. Therefore, the energy of each frequency is quantized and the quanta are photons. For gravity, the operators that describe the area and volume of each region of surface or space also have a discrete spectrum. Therefore, the area and volume of any part of space are also quantized, and the quanta are elementary spatial quanta. As a result, spacetime has a fundamental quantum granular structure at the Planck scale, clipping the ultraviolet infinity of quantum field theory.

Quantum states of spacetime are theoretically described by mathematical structures called spin networks. Spin networks were originally introduced in abstract form by Roger Penrose and later shown by Carlo Roveri and Lies Molin to derive naturally from the non-perturbative quantization of general relativity. The spin network does not represent the quantum state of the spacetime field, but directly represents the quantum state of the spacetime.

The Causal Sets program is an approach to quantum gravity. The basic principle is that space-time is fundamentally discrete (a set of discrete space-times called elements of a causal set) and that space-time events are related in a partial order. This partial order has a physical meaning of causal relationships between spatiotemporal events.

This program is based on the theorem by David Malament that if there is a bijective map between two past and future spacetimes that preserves the causal structure, then the map is a conformal isomorphism. said. The indefinite fit factor is related to the volume of the region of spacetime. This volume coefficient can be recovered by specifying the volume element of each spacetime.

The volume of a spatiotemporal domain can be found by counting the points within that domain. The first model of four-dimensional supergravity (which does not have a name) was formulated by Dmitri Vasilievich Volkov and Vyacheslav A. Soroka in 1973, with spontaneous supersymmetry for the possibility of realistic models. Emphasized the importance of sexual rupture. In 1976, a minimal version of four-dimensional supergravity (with unbroken local supersymmetry) was constructed in detail by Dan Friedman, Sergio Ferrara, and Peter van Nieuwenhuisen.

In 2019, his three were awarded the Special Breakthrough Prize in Fundamental Physics for their discovery. The key question of whether the spin 3/2 fields are always coupled was solved with his nearly simultaneous publication by Deser and Zumino, who independently proposed a minimum four-dimensional model. It was quickly generalized to many different theories in different dimensions, adding additional (N) supersymmetries. Supergravity theories with N>1 is commonly called extended supergravity (SUEGRA). Some supergravity theories by dimensionality reduction have been shown to be related to specific higher-dimensional supergravity theories (example N=1, 11-dimensional supergravity is reduced to T7, 4-dimensional, uncalibrated, N=8 supergravity). The resulting theory was sometimes called the Karza-Klein theory, because in 1919 Karza and Klein constructed a five-dimensional theory of gravity.

Black Holes

Now we're going to see one of the most fascinating mysterious strangest celestial bodies in the universe which is a black hole. Any discussion topic related to space or the universe is incomplete without t black hole.

Most research scientists are in the field of cosmology just because they were fascinated by the nature of the black hole. And also, black holes are complex objects in the universe to understand. Black holes are an important aspect of the celestial bodies of the universe. Its mysterious nature is still unknown to us, most research scientists are working to find out what exactly is in the black hole or if human beings will survive colliding into a black hole.

These are some of the interesting questions about the celestial body which is a black hole now we are going to dig to get them out and study the fundamentals and the important points of the black hole in this chapter. While studying black holes we have to you can limit the thinking of our brain just because studying cosmology at a deeper level would require a great sense and logical reasoning behind it. One could not study cosmology in the deeper aspects of space having a Limited mindset. We have to go beyond our limits and intellectual to learn different things and the working of the universe.

Now coming to the nature of the black hole it has a great pull of gravity no that no object in the universe can safely pass beside a black hole. Any type of celestial body which has a mass greater than our Earth on bigger than that can be easily attracted toward the black hole. Light travels at a speed of nearly 3 lakh km per second but in front of the gravity of the black hole, even light cannot pass. Also, the light photons are squeezed into the black hole. So now you might have a general idea of how strong the gravity of a black hole is. There are different types of parameters by which we can describe the nature and the fundamental of a black hole.

Once a celestial object is gone into a black hole never comes out. So, there is a kind of information lost when a celestial object enters a black hole and further, we can classify the dimensions of a black hole are not same as three-dimensional. A black hole is considered to be one-dimensional and beyond that, there is a factor present which is called the singularity. Singularity can also be defined as the point source of a black hole which is fundamentally called the one-dimensional point of a black hole.

We can't say how many dimensions are present at a time in the black hole but the most probable answer is One dimension. There are millions of black holes present in the entire observable universe ranging from Stellar to intermediate and from intermediate to supermassive black holes, similarly one of the supermassive black holes is present in the center of the Milky Way galaxy. Massive earth-like planets stars and even entire galaxies could fit inside a Black hole. Black holes are this massive. And once an object enters the black hole it has no return into the normal universe which we might call the observable universe.

Coming to the actual physical nature of the black hole the first we will consider is the Event Horizon which is called the boundary of a black hole if an object passes this boundary, it has no return, surely the gravity of a black hole would drag the body into it. So, we should be away from the event horizon if, possible to avoid the pull from the black hole. There could be as many as millions of black holes in the entire galaxy. The size of the black holes is much more than a normal star in the universe. As we discussed earlier a supermassive black hole is present in the center of the galaxy, which can dialect the whole energy mass distribution of the entire galaxy.

Now let us go into the Deep mysteries and theories of the black hole. there are types of energies present in the universe and a black hole or its radiation has the capacity or change the distribution of energy.

As we know a black hole emits radiation and radiation can be electromagnetic in nature and travels in all possible directions in the universe. Thus, the emitted radiation of the black hole can radiate with the direct wave of electromagnetic pulses. There are different theories on black holes that suggest that black could be a way to enter into another dimension or into another possible universe. Because no one knows what's inside a Black hole.

The smallest black hole can range up to 3 to 4 times that of a sun. And the biggest black hole that scientists have founded is about 16 billion times the mass of the sun. The black hole nearest to that of the earth is 1600 light years away from us. The location of the black hole can be predicted by the interaction of radiation and time through its mass. There are different types of waves present in the universe such as electromagnetic radiation through visible light. There are different types of matter present in the universe. If anyone of it goes inside a black hole, it forms an accretion disc.

While discussing black holes We will also focus on the quasars which are the brightest known objects in the universe, which are formed by the emitted radiation from a black hole. Consider a star moving close to that of a black hole, due to the strong gravity of the black hole, all the light of the star will be pulled towards the black hole, and Star will eventually fade. And, generally, the mass of the black hole will increase.

In other words, we can say that the star gets swallowed by the black hole. This proves the amount of gravity A blackhole is having. There are different types of stars orbiting the black hole in place we called as a binary system. A large number of radio waves are emitted from this region. Through its interactions with other stuff and electromagnetic radiation like visible light, black holes can be detected.

Any material that falls into a black hole has the potential to create an exterior accretion disc that is heated by friction and gives rise to quasars, some of the brightest objects in the universe. Supermassive black holes can shred stars into streamers that shine brilliantly before being "swallowed" if they are approached too closely. If there are stars orbiting a black hole, the mass and position of the black hole can be determined from the stars' orbits. By making such findings, one can rule out potential alternatives like neutron stars. This has allowed astronomers to identify a large number of stellar black hole candidates in binary systems, as well as prove the existence of the radio source Sagittarius A.

Albert Einstein created his theory of general relativity in 1915 after demonstrating earlier that gravity does affect the velocity of light. Karl Schwarzschild solved the Einstein field equations that explain the gravitational field of a point mass and a spherical mass only a few months later. Johannes Droste, a Hendrik Lorentz student, independently provided the identical answer for the point mass a few months after Schwarzschild and went into greater detail regarding its characteristics. At what is now known as the Schwarzschild radius, this solution exhibited odd behaviour when it become singular, which meant that some of the terms in the Einstein equations turned infinite.

At the time, it was unclear exactly what kind of surface this was. Arthur Eddington demonstrated in 1924 that the singularity vanished when the coordinates were altered (see Eddington-Finkelstein coordinates), but it wasn't until 1933 that Georges Lemaître understood that this indicated the Schwarzschild radius singularity was a non-physical coordinate singularity. In a book published in 1926, Arthur Eddington did address the possibility of a star with mass compressed to the Schwarzschild radius, noting that Einstein's theory allows us to rule out excessively high densities for visible stars like Betelgeuse because "a star of 250 million km radius could not possibly have so high a density as the Sun."

The no-hair theory states that a black hole only has three independent physical properties once it reaches a stable state after formation: mass, electric charge, and angular momentum; the black hole is otherwise featureless. If the hypothesis is correct, any two black holes with the same values for these parameters are identical and cannot be distinguished from one another. It is currently unknown to what extent the conjecture holds true for actual black holes under the laws of contemporary physics. These characteristics stand out because they can be seen from outside of a black hole.

A charged black hole, for instance, repels other charged objects just like any other charged object. The gravitational equivalent of Gauss's law (through the ADM mass), applied distant from the black hole, can also be used to determine the total mass inside a sphere containing a black hole.

The gravitomagnetic field can also be used to detect angular momentum (or spin) from a distance, for example, through the Lense-Thirring effect. Any details about the geometry of the object or the distribution of charge on it are evenly scattered throughout the black hole's horizon when an object enters it, rendering them invisible to viewers outside the black hole. The membrane paradigm, which describes the behaviour of a conductive stretchy membrane with friction and electrical resistance, is a dissipative system that closely resembles the membrane in this condition.

This contrasts with other field theories like electromagnetism, which are time-reversible and do not exhibit friction or resistivity at the microscopic level. There is no way to prevent losing knowledge of the starting conditions because a black hole eventually achieves a stable state with only three parameters.

The most basic static black holes are massless; they lack both angular momentum and electric charge. Schwarzschild black holes are the name given to these black holes in honour of Karl Schwarzschild, who discovered this answer in 1916. It is the only spherically symmetric vacuum solution, according to

Birkhoff's theorem. This indicates that there is no discernible difference between the gravitational field of a black hole like this one and that of any other spherical object with the same mass from a distance. Therefore, the prevalent belief that a black hole "sucks in everything" in its surroundings is only true when the black hole is close to its horizon; otherwise, the external gravitational field is the same as any other body with the same mass when the black hole is far away.

An event horizon, a border in spacetime through which matter and light may only pass inward toward the black hole's mass, is what distinguishes a black hole from other objects.

Nothing can escape the event horizon, not even light. The reason the event horizon is so named is that if an event takes place inside the boundary, information from it cannot be obtained by an outside observer, making it impossible to know whether such an event actually took place. General relativity states that the presence of a mass causes spacetime to distort in a way that causes particle pathways to bend in the direction of the mass. [83] There are no escape routes from a black hole due to the deformation that occurs at the event horizon of a black hole. A clock near a black hole would appear to tick more slowly to a distant observer than a clock farther away. An item falling into a black hole will appear to slow down as it approaches the event horizon and take an infinite amount of time to get there because of this gravitational time dilation effect.

The falling object eventually disappears until it is no longer visible. Usually, this process moves quite quickly, with an object leaving the field of view in under a second. On the other hand, unharmed viewers entering a black hole are not affected by any of these phenomena as they pass through the event horizon.

They cross the event horizon after a finite amount of time without observing any singular behaviour, according to their own clocks, which appear to them to be ticking normally. In classical general relativity, it is impossible to determine the location of the event horizon from local observations because of Einstein's equivalence principle. In general relativity, singularities are frequently interpreted as signs that the theory is about to fall apart. But given the incredibly high density and resulting particle interactions, this breakdown is to be expected since it occurs in a context where quantum processes should describe these behaviours. Although there have been attempts to develop a theory of quantum gravity, it has not yet been able to integrate quantum and gravitational processes into a single theory. Such a theory is typically predicted to be devoid of singularities.

Metaphysics

Metaphysics is considered to be greatest term in philosophy. The term metaphysics is nothing but existence of particular factor which is parameterized in nature. It is now one of the largest areas of philosophy. There are certain areas in which metaphysics is hard to reach and also some areas I which it has its own importance over there. The ontology and modality of metaphysics is ongoing simultaneously in the part of reality. We will understand metaphysics with some great and existing factors which will allow us to determine the exact definition of it.

Considering the first factor which is Identity, this makes it more reliable in consideration with different universal topics and help us to know more. Whereas metaphysics doesn't deal with ethics and morality just because it's slightly different than what we called as personal identity.

Each and every thing in this universe to go under state of metaphysics requires some of parameters to get classified so we can't call metaphysics as a knowledge for the justification for thing which is existing in the universe. It requires some true facts and methodologies to count it under metaphysics. Travel and reality can be considered as strong troops for metaphysics which does not allow methods of science and theories of Mathematics to interfere with each other Theories which have Particular meaning that is initiated with the universe cannot be accepted as metaphysics. Thus, we need some strong proof for the belief of metaphysics.

The list of areas that metaphysics couldn't cover is equal to list of areas in which matter physics is present. Another definition of metaphysics can be understanding the nature to its fullest. The term metaphysics was first put forth by the Great philosophy learner of all the time Aristotle metaphysics was the name of the first philosophical book written by Aristotle.

The name of the book was given by the publisher who published the first philosophical book by Aristotle in which it is explained that metaphysics is the connection between mind and body, what is the exact connection of mind and body and in what way they are connected to each other are some of the terms explained in the book. As we discussed before there are some parameters metaphysics deals with, one of them is cause and effect, which plays an important role in knowing the exact personality and nature of what we are experiencing.

The root of metaphysics is universe, mind and body, connection of our mind to know the existence of what is in the nature. Getting answers to questions like is there a creator who created this reality what's the difference between the reality and existence we are experiencing in our day today life. There are some of the powerful questions that sets the definition of metaphysics. As we know this book generally deals with the universe and cosmological terms will just try to relate metaphysics in terms of Universal parameters. So, there is a big question in cosmology, is there a creator? Metaphysics tries to solve discretion by giving some philosophical evidences that there might be a creator getting to the higher levels of Universal constant we might get the answer to this question. Metaphysics also deals with the question what is the nature of the consciousness. This is nothing but a form of energy which is present from the beginning of the universe. At the time of the Big Bang, it is believed that the one who plays an important role as observer was consciousness according to the quantum mechanics unless and until we don't see through our eyes everything behaves as a waveform but when the observer is introduced the waveform get or solid shape and the universe is generated and manipulated according to the observer.

Thus, knowing the nature of consciousness it will help us know that who created the universe or who acted as observer at the time of Big Bang.

Many people at that time thought that the definition of the meta physics is nothing but giving the evidences of a particular event after it has been occurred. So many of them denied the term metaphysics but at that time it was the only scientific parameter which helped philosophy to deal with science and technology. Because of this people were forced to ask questions on existence, evidences of reality and many more. This created a great hype and concerns like are we real. We can even consider metaphysics as different branches of space and time. It also questions the existence of God, as we have described consciousness before, we can scientifically prove that consciousness can be God. The source of positive energy which has spread the entire Universe after the Big Ben can be considered as God. So, metaphysics is just dealing with the evidences that what actually is true, there are still different experiences upon what is God what is existence and what is the observer, which was present at the time of The Big Bang.

Metaphysical cosmology is a branch of metaphysics that treats the world as a whole of all phenomena in space and time. Historically, it formed a large part of the field alongside ontology, but its role in modern philosophy is more peripheral: its scope was broad and often based on religion. The ancient Greeks did not distinguish between this usage and their cosmic model. Today, however, we are dealing with cosmic issues that go beyond the scope of natural science. It differs from religious cosmology in that it approaches these issues in a philosophical way. Explaining the existence of spirit in a world made mostly of matter is a metaphysical problem of such vast and important importance that it has become a field in itself, the philosophy of the mind.

Substantial dualism is the classical theory that the mind and body are essentially distinct, the mind possessing some of the attributes traditionally attributed to the soul, and an immediate conceptualization of the interaction of the two. present a puzzle. This form of material dualism differs from the dualism of the Eastern philosophical tradition, which assumes a soul.

From their point of view, the soul is ontologically distinct from the spirit. Idealism assumes that no material object exists unless it is perceived, only as perception. Proponents of panpsychism, a form of property dualism, believe that everything has a spiritual dimension, but they do not believe that everything exists in the mind. Neutral monism posits that beings consist of a single substance, which is neither mental nor physical, but capable of both mental and physical aspects or attributes. Hence, it alludes to the two-sided theory. In the last century, materialistic monism, type identity theory, token identity theory, functionalism, reductive physicalism, non-reductive physicalism, elimination materialism, anomalous monism, trait dualism, epiphenomenalism, and the dominant theories, including emergence, have been scientifically inspired.

Determinism is the philosophical thesis that all events, including human perceptions, decisions and actions, are causally determined by an unbroken chain of previous events. It is important that nothing happens that has not yet been decided.

The main consequence of the deterministic claim is that it calls into question the existence of free will. The question of free will is the question of whether rational actors can control their actions and decisions. Addressing this issue requires understanding freedom and causality and determining whether natural laws are causally deterministic. Some philosophers, known as incompatibility, believe that determinism and free will are mutually exclusive. Therefore, if they believe in determinism, they will believe that free will is an illusion, a position known as hard determinism. Advocates range from Baruch Spinoza to Ted Honderich. Henri Bergson defended free will in his dissertation Time and Free Will of 1889. Others called compatibilists (or "soft determinists") argue that the two ideas are coherent.

I believe that we can harmonize Proponents of this view include Thomas Hobbes and many modern philosophers such as John Martin Fisher, Gary Watson, and Harry Frankfurt. Non-compatibility who, accept free will but reject determinism are called libertarians, and the term should not be confused with its political meaning. Robert Kane and Alvin Plantinga are contemporary defenders of this theory. Although highly hypothetical as a philosophical undertaking, metaphysics also has practical applications in most other areas of philosophy, science, and now information technology.

We start with ontologies (objects, properties, classes, space-time systems, etc.) and other metaphysical perspectives on issues such as causality and consequences, and build our own professional theories on top of them. For example, in science, some theories are based on ontological assumptions of matter with properties (such as electrons with electric charges), while others may reject matter entirely (propagation Quantum Field Theory, where the "electrons" in the field become properties of spacetime, etc.). object).

The "social" branches of philosophy such as moral philosophy, aesthetics, and religious philosophy (which produce practical subjects such as ethics, politics, law, art, etc.) all require a metaphysical foundation that can be viewed as branches. will do. Or the application of metaphysics. For example, we can postulate the basic existence of value, beauty, God, etc.

We then use these assumptions to make our own discussion of the resulting results. As philosophers of these subjects establish their foundations, they can engage in applied metaphysics and utilize core themes and methods, including ontology and other core and peripheral themes, to guide them. As with science, the foundations chosen depend on the underlying ontology, so philosophers of these subjects need to delve into the ontological layers of metaphysics to see what is possible with their theories. Systems engineering is essentially metaphysical and does not acknowledge it.

This is because systems engineering is primarily about understanding what is important in a potential new system. It examines the nature of the situation, also called ontology, and explores the possibilities of measuring, evaluating, identifying, planning, implementing, integrating, testing, and using this epistemology.

Metaphysics keeps asking "why" where science stops. For example, fundamental physics theories are based on a set of axioms that allow us to assume the existence of entities such as atoms, particles, forces, charges, masses, and fields. Setting up such a hypothesis is like considering, the "end" of a scientific theory. Metaphysics takes these hypotheses and examines what they mean as human concepts. For example, do all theories of physics require the existence of space and time, objects and properties? Or can it be expressed in terms of objects only, or properties only? Should objects maintain their identity over time, or can they change? If they change, will they still be the same Is it an object? The theory is that instead of using properties or predicates (e.g``red'') as entities (e.g. redness or redness fields) or processes (properties), some human languages say ``There's redness over there can be reformulated by transforming it into Is the distinction between objects and properties fundamental to the physical world or our perception of it?

Much recent research has been devoted to analyzing the role of metaphysics in the formation of scientific theories.

Alexandre Coile spearheaded this movement, saying in his book Metaphysics and Measurement: "The scientific spirit advances by surpassing rather than following experiment." Metaphysics That propositions can influence scientific theorizing is John Watkins' most enduring contribution to philosophy. Since 1957, he has shown how some non-experimental and therefore non-empirical descriptions of Popper's ideas nevertheless influence the development of a correctly testable and scientific theory. I showed you what you can do. These profound consequences in applied elementary logic. Imre Lakatos argued that all scientific theories have a metaphysical "hard core" that is essential to the generation of hypotheses and theoretical assumptions. According to Lakatos, "relevant scientific changes involve powerful cataclysmic metaphysical revolutions.

Metaphysics also offers a systematic account of the category is employed by physics which can be defined as the study of nature and universe physics is called as a language to understand the universe and different calculations on which we can rely and say it as the development within the philosophy itself.

The traditional concerns of metaphysics are often viewed as problems that arise from the misuse of language for the logical support of statement. we can also say that metaphysics is viewed as applied science metaphysics is also called as a product of the ambiguity is of language it gives better understanding of different concept through which we will get rid of different metaphysical problems.

Regardless of the cause, the range of troubles to which the term metaphysics applies today is so numerous that it is very hard to discover a definition that adequately expresses the character and scope of this subject.

Traditional definitions, which include "trying to find", "trying to describe the truth at the back of all occurrences", and "searching for the primary principles of things" are not only vague and in large part uninformative. It's far neither absolute nor absolute. Faulty: each too broad (relevant to philosophical fields other than metaphysics as properly) or too slender (paradigmically not relevant to metaphysical issues).

The simplest way, therefore, to offer a beneficial account of the nature and quantity of metaphysics as understood these days is to provide an outline of the various philosophical issues which might be surely part of contemporary metaphysics. That trouble belongs totally to trendy (this is, postmedieval) philosophy; no historic or medieval truth seeker a lot as considered any of the questions cited in the preceding paragraph. First explored with the aid of the French philosopher René Descartes (1596–1650), it turned into not appeared as fundamental or in particular essential—that is, as a hassle that every philosophical gadget with any pretense to comprehensiveness was obliged to address—till the work of the Anglo-Irish philosopher George Berkeley (1685–1753) have become widely known.

Berkeley devised very able and innovative arguments for a thoroughgoing form of idealism, consistent with which nothing exists but thoughts (that is sensations and mental photos), things composed of thoughts, and the minds within which ideas exist.

Although few philosophers well-known Berkeley's doctrine—his arguments had been notorious in preference to famous—it changed into commonly taken into consideration essential that it have to be refuted. The standard attitude of philosophers of the 18th century to the hassle of the truth of the external world turned into properly summarized with the aid of the German Enlightenment logician Immanuel Kant (1724–1804), who wrote (in a footnote to the introduction of the second one version [1787] of his Critique of his natural motive.

The awesome revival of metaphysics amongst analytic philosophers in the closing region of the 20th century did nothing to reawaken hobby within the query of the fact of the outside international. Subsequent analytic metaphysics changed into worried either with troubles that had no referring to that query (example, problems regarding modality, ontology, and the nature of time) or with questions on the metaphysics of the bodily or fabric world. (Metaphysicians writing at the metaphysics of the fabric world were content to take its lifestyles as a right and have devoted themselves totally to questions about the sorts of gadgets it comprises and their properties.

Among psychophysical dualists, dualistic interactionists hold that the frame and the mind have interaction—that the thoughts causally affect the frame and the body causally influences the thoughts. Dualistic interactionists seem to be devoted to the location that the physical international is not causally closed which means that bodily activities can't constantly be completely explained with the aid of reference to in advance bodily occasions and the laws of physics. That role, but might appear to be inconsistent with the conservation legal guidelines (conservation of power and conservation of momentum) which might be essential to fashionable physics.

Different psychophysical dualists, referred to as occasionalists, have maintained that the plain causal interaction between thoughts and body is most effective obvious: intellectual and physical adjustments are coordinated by way of the direct action of God. (Therefore, the act of inclined to move one's arm is an "occasion," but no longer a motive, of the motion of 1's arm.) Like interactionists, however, occasionalists seem to be committed to the thesis that there are physical activities that cannot be explained in phrases of earlier physical events.

The principle of preestablished harmony, because of Gottfried Wilhelm Leibniz (1646–1716), in a few ways resembles occasionalism but avoids the hassle of inconsistency with the closure of the bodily international by using postulating separate bodily and intellectual nation-states, each of which unfolds deterministically with the passage of time according to its own laws; the two nation-states do no longer have interaction but had been created (by using God) in any such manner that they may be in perfect concord with each different.

Many philosophers have believed that, similarly to specific matters, there are "fashionable" things of which particular things are times or examples or instances. They have got believed, for instance, that, further to specific horses, the world consists of the species Equus caballus, a fashionable element of which every horse is an instance (and of which only horses are instances). The Latin phrase for such well known things is universalia (singular universale).

Astrobiology

Astrobiology is nothing but a stream which deals with the microorganisms and living things which are apart from our Earth. Anything which is intergalactic or any living beings which are present on different planets of the different solar systems in different galaxies comes under astrobiology. we can also define their Origin by the evolution of the microorganisms and their distribution among different galaxies which may be true. Astro Biology also deals with the future of microorganisms and living things in the universe it also contains some deterministic situations and different kinds of events which Rises when we called life. Astro biology is used in in many different waves such as biochemistry, physical, cosmology, astronomy, chemistry and many different things by which we can directly find the possibility of life in the different world. In other words, we can say that, anything that concerns with life in the outer space fascinates the scientist and they can work in proper way to find out the possibility of life in other galaxies. The origin of life on earth considering the evolution is different, the rate of evolution is different in all the following systems of the entire Galaxy.

Astrobiology deals with extraterrestrial beings. There are different interpretations for proving the life on other planets which comes with some existing scientific data, though astrobiology can be considered as theoretical concept it has some serious theories that this stuff can be true out somewhere in different galaxies. There are some theories which suggest that Astro biology for biochemistry came into existence just after the big bang, which was considered as the habitable space for subatomic particles. To live the habitable approach of the universe, it came when the universe was on the 17millions of age.

There are, different type of hypothesis that, we can consider while learning astrobiology First is Panspermia which tells us that life in different galaxies and solar systems were formed by asteroids and meteorites and many other different small celestial bodies According to research which was published in August 2015 suggest that the galaxies which are more in size are favorable for sustaining life programs.

Research on the origins of planetary systems, the origins of organic compounds in space, rock-water-carbon interactions, abiogenesis on Earth, planetary habitability, studies on biosignatures for life detection, and the potential for life to adapt to difficulties on Earth and in space are all included in this interdisciplinary field.

It has been suggested that life may perhaps be thriving on many of the alien bodies in the universe as a result of developments in the fields of astrobiology and observational astronomy as well as the discovery of numerous extreme-environment-adapted organisms. The search for life on Mars is a special focus of current astrobiology study due to this planet's proximity to Earth and geological history. A rising body of data indicates that Mars once possessed a significant amount of water on its surface, which is thought to be a necessary precondition for the emergence of carbon-based life.

Some simplifying presumptions are helpful in the search for life on worlds other than Earth because they help the astrobiologist's task become more manageable. One is the educated supposition that all life on Earth and the great majority of living forms in our galaxy are built on carbon chemistry. The exceptionally vast diversity of molecules that can form around carbon is well recognized. The energy needed to form or break a bond with carbon, the fourth most abundant element in the universe, is precisely right for creating molecules that are both reactive and stable. Because carbon atoms easily form bonds with one another, it is possible to construct incredibly lengthy and intricate chains.

Biology cannot assert that a process or phenomenon must forcibly exist in an extraterrestrial body just because it is technically conceivable.

What is speculative and what is not is defined by biologists. In order to understand four aspects of the limits of life in a planetary context—the possibility of panspermia, forward contamination as a result of human exploration endeavours, planetary colonization by humans, and the exploration of extinct and extant extraterrestrial life—astrobiologists turned to the discovery of extremophiles. organisms able to survive in extreme environments. Astroecology studies how life on planets, asteroids, and comets interacts with the surroundings and resources of space. Astroecology is the study of the resources for life that are found in stars throughout the galaxy and into the cosmological future. This subject of astrobiology is addressed by a field of study called astrocology.

Using actual space materials found in meteorites, experimental astroecology examines resources in planetary soils. The findings imply that carbonaceous chondrite and Martian materials can support bacterial, algal, and plant (potato, asparagus) cultures with high soil fertility.

The findings suggest that early wet asteroids could have supported life and that comparable materials brought to Earth by meteorites, comets, and dust could be utilized as soil for future space colonies. Understanding life, the kind of settings that support it, planetary, planetary system, and stellar interactions and processes are all necessary for the hunt for life beyond Earth. Astrobiology integrates concepts and methods from a wide range of disciplines, such as astronomy, biology, chemistry, geology, atmospheric science, oceanography, and aeronautical engineering, in order to provide this insight. While astrobiologists from many scientific fields frequently collaborate to study complicated topics that no one field can fully address on its own. Astrobiologists can work alone on specific scientific questions.

Despite being a relatively new topic, astrobiology has a bright future. Astrobiology research has a substantial impact on how organizations like the European Space Agency and the National Aeronautics and Space Administration (NASA) plan for present and future space missions. For instance, numerous recent missions, such as Mars (Phoenix, Pathfinder, Global Surveyor, and others) and Titan, have been tasked with searching for clues of past, present, or the precursors of life on these worlds in our own solar system (Cassini-Huygens).

Researchers may now start organizing and looking for habitable planets outside of our solar system because to considerable developments and investments in telescope technology (Kepler, James Webb Space Telescope).

The discovery of extrasolar planets (planets around other stars), the strong suspicion that several moons of Jupiter and Saturn may have vast reserves of liquid water, and the existence of microorganisms known as extremophiles that are tolerant of environmental extremes have all increased the possibility that biota may be a common feature of the universe, even though no convincing evidence of extraterrestrial life has yet been found.

The first development suggests that there may be a large number of habitats for life. The second postulates that there might be other worlds with life already existing within our solar system. The third asserts that a variety of circumstances can lead to the emergence of life.

A few of the moons of Jupiter, chiefly Europa but also Ganymede and Calisto, as well as Saturn's moon Enceladus, may harbour long-lived liquid seas beneath their frozen exteriors, according to discoveries made mostly by the Galileo space mission (launched in 1989). Gravitational interactions between the moons and their home planet allow these oceans to remain warm despite being far from the Sun, and they may even be able to support the same type of life that can be found in deep sea vents on Earth.

On its chilly surface, where lakes of liquid methane and ethane may exist, even Titan, a massive moon of Saturn with a dense atmosphere, may harbour some strange biology. Indicators of liquid flow were observed on Titan's surface by the European spacecraft Huygens after it touched down there in January 2005. By expanding the spectrum of potential alien habitats well beyond the usual concept of a "habitable zone," such discoveries have significantly aided the formation of astrobiology as a field of study.

The 1995 finding of hundreds of extrasolar planets orbiting other sun-like stars has provided further incentive. The majority of these are massive worlds, similar to Jupiter, making them unlikely to be habitable, however they might have moons on them. However, recent research has revealed that at least 5 to 10% (and probably as much as 50% or more) of all Sun-like stars have planets, suggesting that the Milky Way Galaxy has many billions of solar systems. The discovery of these planets has sparked interest in astrobiology, and in particular, proposals for several space-based telescopes have been made. These telescopes are intended to (1) look for smaller, Earth-sized worlds, and (2), if such worlds are discovered, to analyse spectrally the light reflected by the planets' atmospheres in the hope of finding oxygen, methane, or other compounds that would suggest the presence of biota.

Astrobiology aims to comprehend both the potential for extraterrestrial life in the universe as well as the possibility for life to continue on some other moons and planets in our own solar system. It also looks into the possibility of life adapting to harsh settings, such as those found in outer space or on other planets or moons. Searching for water and livable habitats on other planets, looking for biomarkers (evidence of life) on other planetary systems, and examining the ability for life to adapt to harsh environments are some of the major research subjects in astrobiology.

Searching for suitable habitats and water on other worlds, looking for indicators (signs of life) on other heavenly bodies, and examining the capacity for life to adapt to harsh conditions are some of the major research subjects in astrobiology.

Extraterrestrials

Extraterrestrial life, often known as alien life, is life that may exist outside of Earth and that did not develop there. Although studies are in progress, no conclusive evidence of extraterrestrial life has yet been found. From primitive forms like prokaryotes to sophisticated creatures, this life could give rise to civilizations that are considerably more developed than our own. The Drake equation makes assumptions regarding the possibility of intelligent life existing elsewhere in the cosmos. Astrobiology is the study of alien life.

Pre-modern authors frequently made the assumption that extraterrestrial "worlds" would contain live creatures. In the fifteenth century, William Vorilong acknowledged that Christ might have travelled to other planets to save the people who lived there. The Earth, according to Nicholas of Cusa, was "a brilliant star" like other celestial objects visible in space in 1440. From the outside, this "fiery brightness" in the outer layer of the atmosphere would make the Earth appear comparable to the Sun. He proposed that humans, plants, and animals might live on every alien body, including the Sun. Descartes claimed that it was only speculation as to whether or not "intelligent entities" lived among the stars and that there was no way to definitively verify their existence.

Extraterrestrial life, and especially extraterrestrial intelligence, have had a significant cultural impact, notably in fiction. Science fiction has shared scientific concepts over time, envisaged a wide range of scenarios, and shaped public perceptions of extraterrestrial life. The argument about whether it is wise to try to contact extraterrestrial intelligence is one shared space. Some advocate using forceful techniques to look for intelligent extraterrestrial life. Others say that it could be risky to actively draw attention to Earth, citing the propensity of technologically sophisticated human nations to enslave or wipe out less advanced societies.

Microorganisms and other forms of extraterrestrial life have been theorised to exist in the Solar System and elsewhere in the universe. This idea is supported by the observable universe's enormous size and constant physical laws. This line of thinking is shared by scientists like Carl Sagan and Stephen Hawking, who contend that it is highly unlikely that life does not exist elsewhere than Earth. The Copernican principle and the mediocrity principle both support this claim that Earth does not hold a special place in the universe and therefore life on Earth is not particularly noteworthy.

Astronomers have suggested that "habitable zones" around stars are the most plausible locations for the existence of life since the 1950s. Since 2007, there have been numerous discoveries of these zones, leading to numerical estimates of many billions of planets with Earth-like compositions. Only a few planets had been found in these regions as of 2013. However, on November 4, 2013, astronomers announced that the number of Earth-sized planets in the habitable zones of Sun-like stars and red dwarfs in the Milky Way might reach 40 billion, with 11 billion of those planets possibly orbiting Sun-like stars, based on data from the Kepler space mission. Scientists estimate that the closest such planet may be 12 light-years away.

An environment with non-equilibrium thermodynamics, in which the thermodynamic equilibrium must be disturbed by a source of energy, is the first fundamental prerequisite for life.

The stars have traditionally been thought of as the universe's primary energy sources. For example, life on Earth depends on the sun's energy. However, there are additional sources of alternative energy, including hydrothermal vents, volcanoes, and plate tectonics. On Earth, there are ecosystems at the depths of the ocean that don't get sunlight but instead get their energy from black smokers. Although these would be, less effective sources of energy, magnetic fields and radiation have also been mentioned.

Water must be in a liquid condition in order for biological reactions to occur in order for life to exist. An abiogenesis process is exceedingly unlikely to begin in a gaseous or solid medium because the atom speeds, which can be either too rapid or too slow, make it challenging for specific ones to meet and initiate chemical reactions. It is also possible to transport nutrients and other things needed for metabolism in a liquid medium. On terrestrial planets with a chemical composition and temperature range similar to that of Earth, the development of living beings may be possible if there is an adequate supply of water, carbon, and other components. Ammonia-based life has been proposed as an alternative to water-based life, albeit this solvent seems less suited.

Extraterrestrial life may have a fundamentally different biochemistry even if it is carbon-based and uses water as a solvent, like Earth life. RNA was the first form of life on Earth, and when it evolved into its current state, some of the functions performed by RNA were passed to DNA and proteins. It's possible that extraterrestrial life will either remain fixed on the RNA planet or evolve into different forms. It is unknown which elements would exhibit a similar pattern or if our biochemistry is the most effective one that could be produced. However, it is conceivable that cells would still have a cell membrane even if they were made of materials other than those found on Earth.

Through evolution, life on Earth transitioned from prokaryotes to eukaryotes and from unicellular to multicellular creatures. No alternative method, even one that is purely hypothetical, has yet been thought of to accomplish such a result. Because of evolution, life must be separated into distinct creatures, and no viable alternative structure has been put forth. At the most fundamental level, a cell's membranes define the boundary between it and its surroundings while still allowing for some energy and resource exchange.

It is not certain how eukaryotes, which are multicellular lifeforms, evolved from basic cells. Thousands of millions of years after the beginning of life, the Cambrian explosion occurred, and its origins are still not completely understood.

Simon Conway Morris, a palaeontologist, believes that convergent evolution would result in kingdoms that are similar to our own plants and animals. He also believes that many characteristics, such as bilateral symmetry, limbs, digestive systems, and heads with sensory organs, are likely to develop in alien animals. A planet with more gravity would have smaller animals, and various kinds of stars may result in non-green photosynthesizers. The planetary setting would also play a role. The amount of energy available would also have an impact on biodiversity because an ecosystem supported by hydrothermal vents or black smokers would have less energy available than one supported by a star's light and heat, which would prevent its lifeforms from evolving past a certain level of complexity.

Some worlds in the Solar System, especially those that may have underground oceans, may provide a habitat for extraterrestrial life. Astrobiologists predict that if life is found beyond in the Solar System, it will likely take the form of extremophile microbes. The 2015 Astrobiology Strategy from NASA states that "life on other worlds is most likely to contain microbes, and any complex living system elsewhere is likely to have originated from and be based upon microbial life.

Studies of bacteria on current Earth, as well as their ubiquity and ancestral traits, can provide important information on the limits of microbial life. Deep underground, scientists discovered a startling variety of subterranean species, predominantly microbes. They estimate that the Earth's crust is home to roughly 70% of all bacteria and archaea organisms. "I think it's probably reasonable to assume that the subsurface of other planets and their moons are habitable, especially since we've seen here on Earth that organisms can function far away from sunlight using the energy provided directly from the rocks deep underground," said Rick Colwell, a member of the Deep Carbon Observatory team from Oregon State University, to the BBC.

There is proof that Mars was wetter and warmer in the past: There have been discoveries of dried-up riverbeds, polar ice caps, volcanoes, and minerals that form in the presence of water. The Curiosity rover's 2013 analysis of Aeolis Palus in Gale Crater yielded evidence that strongly points to the existence of an old freshwater lake that would have provided a favourable habitat for microbial life. Additionally, current Martian subsurface conditions may be able to sustain life.

Astrobiology, the study of extraterrestrial life, is a branch of science entirely. This field, also known as exobiology, is researched by the NASA, ESA, INAF, and other organisations. Astrobiology is the study of life outside of Earth, but from a cosmic viewpoint. For instance, the possibility of abiogenesis occurring in other celestial bodies is of interest to astrobiology rather than the beginning of life on Earth. From its definition to its chemistry, many facets of life are examined and classified as either being unique to Earth or likely to be shared by all life forms throughout the cosmos.

The 20th century saw significant technological advancements, predictions of possible future technologies, and a rise in the general public's basic understanding of science as a result of science communication through the media. Pseudosciences that offered affirmative, albeit dubious, explanations for the presence of extraterrestrial life emerged in response to the public's curiosity in extraterrestrial life and the absence of discoveries by mainstream science. According to ufology, many unidentified flying objects (UFOs) are spacecraft from extraterrestrial species, and the ancient astronaut hypothesis contends that aliens visited Earth in antiquity and prehistory but that no one could have understood them because of human ignorance at the time. The majority of reported sightings of UFOs or UFOs can be easily accounted for as sightings of Earth-based aircraft, including top-secret aircraft, well-known celestial objects.

Nobody is certain which characteristics of living systems are necessary, meaning that they must exist in all living systems, and which are contingent, meaning that they are the product of evolutionary accidents, meaning that in another location, a different chain of events may have produced different characteristics of life. In this regard, the discovery of even a single instance of extraterrestrial life—no matter how simple in structure or composition—would signify a profound shift in the field of science. Does the universe have a wide variety of biological themes and counterpoints, or are there locations with live fugues, in comparison to which Earth's one melody seems a little thin and reedy?

Nobody is certain which characteristics of living systems are necessary, meaning that they must exist in all living systems, and which are contingent, meaning that they are the product of evolutionary accidents, meaning that in another location, a different chain of events may have produced different characteristics of life. In this regard, the discovery of even a single instance of extraterrestrial life—no matter how simple in structure or composition—would signify a profound shift in the field of science.

Does the universe have a wide variety of biological themes and counterpoints, or are there locations with live fugues, in comparison to which Earth's one melody seems a little thin and reedy? Or is Earth's music the only one available?

It is possible to approach these topics using a variety of criteria. The cosmic abundance of the main atoms should be higher than average. At the temperature of the planet in question, the structural molecules of creatures shouldn't be so very stable as to make chemical processes impossible, but they also shouldn't be incredibly unstable as to cause the organism to disintegrate. There must be a medium for molecular interaction.

Solids should not be used due to their inertness. The medium must be stable in a number of ways. It is most likely a liquid but might also be a highly dense gas.

It ought to have a wide range of temperatures (for a liquid, the temperature difference between freezing point and boiling point should be large). It should be challenging to vaporise and freeze the liquid, as well as challenging to adjust the liquid's temperature in general. An excellent solvent must be present in the interaction medium. The planet in question must have a fluid phase because material must cycle from the creature to the environment as food and waste.

As a result, the planet ought to have an atmosphere and some liquid close to the surface, though perhaps not an ocean of water. There is a wide range of potential outcomes for life on distant planets. It's possible for a planet to be devoid of all organic remains and fossils. It could also be dead but still contain organic material or fossils. There could be simple or extremely complicated biochemistry, physiology, and behaviour in life. It's possible to find sentient life with a technological civilization. Any of these options would require confirmation, which would be very significant for science.

The best way to understand the quest for extraterrestrial life is to picture it in reverse. For instance, if there were people on Mars, they might examine Earth for life using all of the available scientific instruments and expertise. Testing could be done on-site and remotely. Any wavelength of light emitted or reflected by the target planet can be analysed during remote testing. Remote sensing techniques look for thermodynamic disequilibrium, particularly in the planet's liquid phases (atmosphere and hydrosphere). When doing in situ studies, apparatus that lands on a planet and conducts experiments must collect samples of that planet.

You might also look for chemical, mechanical, or spectral disequilibria. Although the abundance of methane in the Earth's atmosphere should be less than one part in 1035 in thermodynamic equilibrium, it is present in considerable quantities together with molecular oxygen (1.7–2 parts per million (106)). This enormous gap suggests that some process produces methane on Earth continuously and quickly, increasing its steady-state abundance to an extremely high level before it can be oxidised. Although the mechanism for the methane disequilibrium need not be biological (for example, relatively stable aromatic hydrocarbons could have been created early in Earth's history without the use of living organisms, and slow degradation may then have led to a continuous loss of methane from the planetary subsurface), a biological explanation seems more likely.

The methane disparity could be viewed as an early sign of life on Earth, as seen from Mars. Indeed, microorganisms are to blame for the high levels of methane on Earth. Some methanogenic bacteria are found in marshes (thus the name "marsh gas" for methane), while others are found in the ruminant's digestive systems, such as cows.

The abundance of free oxygen gas could also be seen as a sign of life. It would be necessary to rule out the notion that oxygen originates from the photodissociation of water and the consequent escape of hydrogen into space. Additionally, terpenes—hydrocarbons released by plants and found over forests—which are rather complicated reduced organic compounds, could be detected using spectroscopy as a test for life.

The majority of life's exams are inherently vague. Contamination continues to be a constant issue. Any spacecraft could transport living things from the earth and report finding them on the target planet. To ensure that the spacecraft is thoroughly cleaned and doesn't carry any life from Earth, great care must be taken.

Even the discovery of large amounts of extraterrestrial organic materials may be deceptive. Carbonaceous chondrite meteorites from the asteroid belt strike the planet. They have up to 4% mass of organic stuff. It has been determined that this material does not have a biological origin. Subsequent research refuted claims that living microorganisms might be extracted from the interiors of carbonaceous chondrites. Because they are porous, these meteorites "breathe" air in and out both when they enter the atmosphere and when they are stored until being studied. The abundance of microbes provides significant chances for contamination after their arrival on Earth. There were some facultative aerobes found in bacteria recovered from a meteorite. It seems implausible that the electron-transfer multienzyme pathways necessary for oxygen respiration originated in the asteroid belt since no planet in the solar system other than Earth contains considerable amounts of oxygen gas.

There isn't one clear-cut "life detector" in existence. It takes luck or the solution of challenging instrumental issues for instruments of enormous generality that make few uncertain assumptions about the nature of extraterrestrial life, such as the requirement that an animal or protist pass by during the camera's operational lifespan (e.g., the acquisition and preparation of samples for remote electron microscopic examination).

Highly sensitive tools, like metabolism detectors, are aimed for hypothetically much more plentiful organisms than animals. These tools heavily rely on hypotheses, which are essentially educated guesses (e.g., that extraterrestrial organisms eat sugars). Therefore, it is advised to use a variety of extremely broad and very particular instruments to confirm or disprove the existence of extraterrestrial life in the solar system.

The potential for life on the planets and moons of the solar system are briefly discussed after that. There are many diverse habitats in the solar system that may provide important hints about the beginning of life and possibly even life itself. A conclusive case for or against extraterrestrial life on these planets does not yet exist, though.

In the past, the "canals" were used to support the existence of life on Mars. This apparent network of thin, straight lines that cuts through the Martian bright regions spans many miles and varies seasonally. The lines were catalogued and made more well-known by American astronomer Percival Lowell around the beginning of the 20th century after being first carefully spotted in 1887 by Italian astronomer Giovanni V. Schiaparelli. Lowell asserted that the lines could not have come from a natural source because of their immaculate straightness. Instead, he saw them as man-made structures created by advanced Martians. They might be canals that transport water from the melting polar caps to the dry equatorial towns, according to Lowell.

Two American probes, Viking 1 and 2, which successfully touched down on Mars in July and August of 1976, carried instruments for locating organic stuff. Results from analyses of air and soil samples were conclusive, and the information was interpreted negatively. There is no sign of life anywhere around these probes, at least. Structures and sedimentary magnetite from the Allan Hills Martian meteorite revealed by research in 1996 have been viewed by some as concrete proof of incredibly minute microbial life on Mars. The majority of scientists, however, are incredibly dubious that the Allan Hills meteorite genuinely includes signs of previous Martian life. The culprits are more likely to be small carbonate crystals and abiogenic magnetite. The hunt for past and present Martian life is still on.

Hydrogen, helium, methane, ammonia, some neon, and water vapour make up Jupiter's atmosphere. Experiments that mimic the early Earth use precisely these gases. The use of energy to replicate Jovian atmospheres has been the subject of computer and lab investigations. Significant amounts of acetylene and hydrogen cyanide are immediate gas-phase products. Lower yields are produced when more complex organic compounds, such as aromatic hydrocarbons, are created. Jupiter's clouds are brightly coloured, and organic chemicals may be to blame for their hue. The apparent absorption characteristic in Jupiter's UV spectrum about 260 nanometers may be caused by aromatic compounds or possibly nucleotide bases.

Although less is known about them, Saturn, Uranus, and Neptune, the other Jovian planets, resemble Jupiter. Their cloud top temperatures drop off as they go further from the Sun. Studies using microwaves on Saturn show that the temperature of the atmosphere rises with depth beneath the clouds. It is anticipated that conditions are similar on Jupiter, Uranus, and Neptune. There are numerous natural satellites connected to these solar system planets. Some have atmospheres, including Io, a satellite of Jupiter, and Titan, a satellite of Saturn. There is currently no proof that life exists on the outer planets or their satellites, despite the relative fitness for life's prerequisites. Organic compounds are present in tens of thousands of comets as well as a small number of asteroids and asteroidal pieces that circle the Sun between Mars and Jupiter. The organic material in the carbonaceous chondrites is thought to have come from asteroids. Pluto has a frozen atmosphere made primarily of nitrogen, carbon dioxide, and methane that covers its surface.

The lack of atmosphere and liquid water on the asteroids and Pluto's extreme cold and sparse solar radiation all militate against the possibility of discovering life there.

Since ancient times, people have questioned whether they are the only species in the cosmos and whether there are other planets with beings that are somewhat similar to humans. The widespread belief during the Middle Ages and the Ancient Planet was that Earth was the only "world" in the universe. Numerous mythology depicted celestial beings in the sky, which is undoubtedly an instance of extraterrestrial life. The Milky Way Galaxy has 200 billion billion stars. The Milky Way Galaxy is roughly 10 billion years old. $R^* = 10$ stars every year is generally a reasonably reliable number. Although the majority of current models of star formation suggest that planets form alongside stars, these theories have not been sufficiently established to warrant much trust. There are more than 250 known extrasolar planets.

They have been noticed in a variety of ways, including: by "wobble," which measures the shift in a star's light's wavelength as it moves from being close to Earth to being further away when a large planet pulls it away from the system's centre; via transit, which measures a star's dimming as a solar eclipse.

Astrophysics

Astrophysics is a science that examines astronomical objects and events using techniques and concepts from physics and chemistry. Astrophysics "seeks to discover the essence of the heavenly bodies, rather than their positions or motions in space—what they are, rather than where they are," as one of the discipline's founders put it. The Sun, other stars, galaxies, extrasolar planets, the interstellar medium, and the cosmic microwave background are some of the topics addressed.

The luminosity, density, temperature, and chemical makeup of these objects' emissions are all investigated across the whole electromagnetic spectrum. Astrophysicists use ideas and techniques from a wide range of physics disciplines, including classical mechanics, electromagnetic, statistical mechanics, and thermodynamics, because the field of astrophysics is so broad.

In reality, theoretical and observational physics-related work is frequently a significant part of current astronomical study. Astrophysicists investigate the origin and ultimate fate of the cosmos, as well as the characteristics of dark matter, dark energy, black holes, and other celestial bodies. The creation and evolution of galaxies, the formation and evolution of the solar system, stellar dynamics and evolution, magnetohydrodynamics, the large-scale structure of the universe's matter, the origin of cosmic rays, general relativity, special relativity, quantum mechanics, and physical cosmology, including string cosmology and astroparticle physics, are all subjects that theoretical astrophysicists also study.

A long time ago, the study of astronomy was separated from the study of terrestrial physics. According to the Aristotelian worldview, celestial bodies appeared to be immovable spheres that only moved uniformly in a circle, whereas the earthly world was seen as a place where growth and decay occurred and where natural motion occurred in a straight line and came to an end when the moving object reached its destination.

As a result, it was believed that the heavenly realm was composed of a substance that was essentially distinct from that of the earthly sphere. This substance was either Fire, as maintained by Plato, or Aether, as maintained by Aristotle. Celestial study was primarily concerned with the regular tasks of determining the locations and computing the movements of astronomical objects for the majority of the nineteenth century. When William Hyde Wollaston and Joseph von Fraunhofer independently discovered that when decomposing the light from the Sun, a multitude of dark lines (regions where there was less or no light) were observed in the spectrum, a new branch of astronomy—soon to be called astrophysics—began to take shape.

By 1860, chemist Robert Bunsen and physicist Gustav Kirchhoff had shown that the dark lines in the solar spectrum matched bright lines in the spectra of well-known gases, with certain lines corresponding to particular chemical components.

Norman Lockyer, who discovered radiant and dark lines in solar spectra in 1868, was one of many who furthered the study of solar and stellar spectra. Together with scientist Edward Frankland, he examined the spectra of several elements at varying pressures and temperatures, but they were unable to connect a yellow line in the solar spectrum to any recognised elements. He therefore asserted that the line represented a brand-new element that was given the name helium in honour of the Greek god of the sun, Helios.

At the Harvard College Observatory, Edward C. Pickering began an extensive programme of stellar spectral classification in 1885. A group of female computers, including Williamina Fleming, Antonia Maury, and Annie Jump Cannon, categorised the spectra captured on photographic plates.

Both electromagnetic theory and relativity theory mention the speed of light in a vacuum (c); in the later, it uses the equation E = mc2 to link energy and mass. Its value is independent of any specific experimental circumstances that can influence the speed of a sound wave in air (for which air temperature and the direction and speed of any wind would matter). It is a fundamental law of nature. The electron has a charge that is essential to all physical particles and is the smallest unit of free electric charge known to exist. Numerous branches of physics and chemistry call for knowledge of this quantity's numerical value, such as for determining the mass of an element or compound released by a specific amount of current flowing through an electrochemical cell.

The universal gravitational constant (G) connects the mass and separation of two bodies to the strength of their gravitational attraction. It is very challenging to experimentally measure its worth. It has been proposed that G is scale-dependent and that it has changed over the course of the universe's history. There is currently no strong evidence that this is the case, but if it were, values found in lab experiments would not be adequate for terrestrial or astronomical concerns.

The physical constants' numerical values vary depending on the unit system in which they are expressed. For instance, the approximate speed of light can be expressed as 186,000 miles per second or 30,000,000,000 centimetres per second. But lately, the units have a tendency to be defined in terms of the physical constants. The distance light travels in a specific amount of time is now the definition of a metre. These definitions are established through worldwide consensus. International System of Units is another option.

The study of astronomical occurrences and objects that release gamma rays is known as gamma-ray astronomy. Gamma-ray telescopes are made to look at high-energy astrophysical objects such stellar coronas, white dwarf stars, neutron stars, black holes, remains of supernovae, galaxy clusters, and diffuse gamma-ray background radiation that is present along the Milky Way Galaxy's plane. High-altitude balloons or spacecraft are typically used to make observations because Earth's atmosphere largely filters off gamma rays. Defense satellites built in the 1960s to find X-rays and gamma rays from covert nuclear testing accidentally found mysterious gamma-ray bursts originating from outer space.

Eliza Hoxie Norris, a proud and talented mathematician, and liberal Presbyterian preacher Alexander Gatherer Russell welcomed their first son, Russell, in 1890. Russell then enrolled at Princeton University in 1893, where he received his top honours in 1897. Russell's greatest intellectual influencers, aside from his family, were the mathematician Henry B. Fine and the astronomer Charles Augustus Young. He earned his Ph.D. from Princeton in 1900 with a thesis that was firmly rooted in conventional mathematical astronomy—an explanation of how Mars perturbs the orbit of the asteroid Eros.

Russell worked at Princeton for almost his whole career. He advanced fast, earning a professorship in 1911 and taking over as observatory director the following year. His major focus was always research; he continued to carry out these administrative duties until his retirement in 1947, but he delegated much of the management of the observatory and the teaching to others.

Stars and their life cycle

An astronomical object known as a star is made up of a bright plasma spheroid that is held together by gravity. The Sun is the star that is closest to Earth. Other stars are also visible at night with the unaided eye, but because to their great distances from Earth, they appear as stationary points of light. Many of the brightest stars have names, and the most notable stars have been grouped into constellations and asterisms. The known stars are included in star catalogues that astronomers have created, and these star catalogues offer conventional stellar designations.

The gravitational collapse of a gaseous nebula made largely of hydrogen, helium, and traces of heavier elements results in the birth of a star. The primary factor influencing its evolution and ultimate fate is its entire mass. The thermonuclear fusion of hydrogen into helium in a star's core is what keeps it glowing for the majority of its active life. As a result of this process, energy is released into space and travels throughout the star's interior. A star's core eventually decomposes into a stellar remnant, such as a white dwarf, neutron star, or black hole if the star is sufficiently massive.

Almost all chemical elements heavier than lithium that are naturally present are produced by stellar nucleosynthesis in stars or their remnants. Chemically enhanced material returns to the interstellar medium as a result of supernova explosions or star mass loss. New stars are created from these recycled components. By making observations of a star's apparent brightness, spectrum, and changes in its position in the sky over time, astronomers can establish stellar attributes such as mass, age, metallicity (chemical composition), variability, distance, and motion across space.

As in the case of planetary systems and star systems with two or more stars, stars can form orbital systems with other celestial objects. The gravitational interaction between two such stars can have a substantial effect on their evolution when they are in reasonably tight orbits. Stars can be a component of a galaxy or star cluster, two considerably bigger gravitationally connected structures. The distinction between "fixed stars," whose location on the celestial sphere is constant, and "wandering stars," or planets, which move visibly in relation to fixed stars over the course of days or weeks, was made by early astronomers. The stars, according to many early astronomers, were thought to be immutably fixed to a heavenly sphere. By convention, notable stars were arranged into asterisms and constellations, and astronomers used these to monitor the motions of the planets and determine the Sun's approximate location. Calendars that might be used to control agricultural activities were made using the motion of the Sun in relation to the background stars (and the horizon).

Since most stellar changes happen too slowly to be noticed, even over a long period of time, it is not possible to study stellar evolution by looking at the life of a single star. Instead, by studying several stars at different stages of their lives and modelling stellar structure with computer models, astrophysicists learn about how stars develop.

A massive molecular cloud collides gravitationally to begin the process of forming stars. Typical huge molecular clouds can contain up to 6,000,000 solar masses (1.21037 kg) and are about 100 light-years (9.51014 km) wide. A massive molecular cloud bursts into ever-tinier fragments as it falls. The compressing gas releases heat from gravitational potential energy in each of these fragments. A fragment condenses into a revolving ball of extremely hot gas known as a protostar as its temperature and pressure rise. The molecular cloud contains a genuinely vast array of filamentary formations.

When a protostar reaches its final mass, it transforms into a pre-main-sequence star by accreting gas and dust from the molecular cloud. Its mass determines further development. Commonly, mass is compared to that of the Sun. When the core temperature of a more massive protostar reaches 10 million kelvin, the proton-proton chain reaction starts, allowing hydrogen to fuse, first into deuterium and later into helium. When nuclear fusion begins, a hydrostatic equilibrium immediately develops in which the energy supplied by the core keeps the gas pressure high, balancing the star's mass and preventing further gravitational collapse. As a result, the star evolves quickly to a stable condition and enters the main-sequence phase. A new star will be located at a given location on the Hertzsprung-Russell diagram's main sequence, with the main-sequence spectral type depending on the star's mass. While large, hot O-type stars will depart the main sequence in just a few million years, small, relatively cold, low-mass red dwarfs will stay there for hundreds of billions of years or more. Similar to the Sun, a medium-sized yellow dwarf star will spend roughly 10 billion years on the main sequence. The main sequence phase, which our Sun is currently in, is the phase that a star enters if it is large enough to fuse hydrogen atoms into helium.

The main sequence phase is when stars spend the majority of their lives. Hydrogen is currently being fused with helium by nuclear fusion. The star's stability is dependent on the light pressure of this energy counteracting the gravitational collapse of the star.

In the universe, main sequence stars make up about nine out of 10 stars. The mass of these stars can range from about a tenth of our Sun's mass to 200 times as massive, and a star's size determines how long it will remain in the main sequence phase. Even if a star with a higher mass has more material to work with, it will burn more quickly because of the higher core temperatures brought on by stronger gravitational pulls. A star the size of our Sun will stay in this phase for approximately 10 billion years, whereas a star 10 times as massive as our own will only remain in it for 20 million years. The star will turn into a red giant after it exits the main sequence phase. In one of the final stages of stellar evolution, a red giant is a dying star.

The Earth may be swallowed up by our dying and expanding Sun in a few billion years, but don't worry—we'll have passed away a few billion years sooner. The temperature of the Earth's surface will rise to levels that are far too high for us humans, even if we do manage to survive for another billion years.)

Nuclear fusion will stop producing helium from hydrogen in stars, and gravity will take control. I'm afraid it's all downhill from here. Red giant stars can grow to 62 million to 621 million miles (100 million to 1 billion kilometres) in diameter, which is 100 to 1,000 times the current sun's size. Similar to how pixels increase in a raster graphic, the star's energy is dispersed over a bigger area. As a result, the star actually cools down and only attains a little bit more than half the heat of the Sun. A red giant gets its name from the fact that as temperature changes, stars begin to shine more reddish-colored light.

However, their helium cores are not large enough to reach the temperatures necessary for helium fusion, therefore they never reach the tip of the red-giant branch. Slightly more massive stars do expand into red giants. These stars travel immediately off the red-giant branch like post-asymptotic-giant-branch (AGB) stars, but at a lower brightness, to become white dwarfs after the hydrogen shell burning is complete.

Convective material is mixed by turbulence from close to the fusing regions up to the star's surface in the expanding outer layers of the star. Prior to now, the fused material had stayed buried deep inside all but the lowest-mass stars.

The red-giant branch's helium core is still expanding. Because it is either degenerate or above the Chandrasekhar limit, it is no longer in thermal equilibrium, and as a result, when its temperature rises, the rate of fusion in the hydrogen shell also rises. The star gets brighter as it gets closer to the red-giant branch's tip.

The core masses and luminosities of red-giant branch stars with a degenerate helium core are all quite similar, although the more massive red giants achieve the helium fusion ignition temperature earlier.

As an alternative, a star with at least eight solar masses will die in a way that is both far more violent and much more beautiful. When a massive star runs out of fuel, a supernova can result. To them, fading away is preferable to going out on top. Supernovae shoot their interiors into space at velocities between 9,000 and 25,000 miles per second when they explode. A neutron star or, in the event of cores that are larger than the Tolman-Oppenheimer, a black hole, will be created when the core of a huge star collapses.

Some of the gravity energy produced by this core collapse is transformed into a Type Ib, Type Ic, or Type II supernova by an unidentified process. Since supernova 1987A, it is known that the core collapse causes a significant increase of neutrinos. The extremely energetic neutrinos break up some nuclei; some of their energy is used to release nucleons, including neutrons, and some of it is converted into heat and kinetic energy, amplifying the shock wave that was initially caused by the rebound of some of the infalling material from the core collapse.

The abundance of elements heavier than iron (and specifically, of sure isotopes of factors which have a couple of stable or lengthy-lived isotopes) produced in such reactions could be very specific from that produced in a supernova, despite the fact that non-exploding purple giants can produce enormous quantities of such elements the use of neutrons released in side reactions of earlier nuclear reactions.

Each, supernovae and the ejection of materials from pink giants are important to provide an explanation for the discovered abundance of heavy elements and isotopes of those elements due to the fact neither abundance by myself fits that located inside the sun system.

By volume, atoms are typically primarily electron clouds with extremely compact nuclei at their centers. Electron capture is the process by which protons and electrons are fused during stellar core collapse due to pressure. The neutrons collide form a dense ball (which resembles a big atomic nucleus in certain aspects) in the absence of electrons, which keep nuclei apart, and are covered in a thin coating of degenerate matter (chiefly iron unless matter of different composition is added later). The Pauli exclusion principle, which is greater than the electron degeneracy pressure, prevents the neutrons from being compressed any further.

That does not imply that the star's remaining components have reached their destination. The star's core is left behind after the supernova explosion and is either left as a black hole or a neutron star, both of which are highly destructive and violently beautiful.

Neutron stars are elusive, cryptic, and difficult to find. Don't be fooled by their size—they may only be roughly the size of a city—because these are dangerous objects. They are incredibly dense; to put it another way, a neutron star has a density that is about equivalent to our sun's mass multiplied by two and then compressed to the size of Los Angeles.

On the other hand, what's left over after the explosion may develop into a black hole. Space is literally pulled away from black holes. For them to have the necessary gravity to draw in light, they must contain a tremendous amount of mass in a very small area. To put this into perspective, the Earth would have to be compressed down to the size of a pea in order to become a black hole!

These enigmatic and terrifying objects have the power to slow down time, tear you apart, and when a black hole reaches its event horizon, nothing can escape its clutches. Anything that crosses its path is lost forever. You, me, and everything else around us are made up of these particles.

The stars are due our lives. You cannot deny that stars are some of the most exquisite and lyrical objects in all of creation, regardless of how big or small, how old or young. Keep in mind that this is how all stars were made and will die the next time you gaze up at the stars.

Type Of Galaxies

A galaxy is a collection of stars, stellar remains, interstellar gas, dust, and dark matter that are gravitationally bonded together.

The name comes from the Greek word galaxias, which means "milky" and refers to the Milky Way galaxy, which houses the Solar System. Galaxies range in size from dwarfs with fewer than 100 million stars to the largest known galaxies, supergiants with one hundred trillion stars around their galaxy's centre of mass. Galaxies are thought to have an average of 100 million stars. Only a small percentage of the mass in a normal galaxy is visible in the form of stars and nebulae; the majority of the galaxy's mass is dark matter. Supermassive black holes are a typical component of galaxy centres.

According on their optical shape, galaxies are classified as elliptical, spiral, or irregular. It's believed that the centres of several of them contain supermassive black holes. Sagittarius A*, the name of the Milky Way's primary black hole, is four million times more massive than the Sun. GN-z11 is the oldest and furthest away galaxy as of March 2016. It can be seen as having existed only 400 million years after the Big Bang and is located 32 billion light-years away from Earth. According to their optical shape, galaxies can be classified as elliptical, spiral, or irregular. It's believed that the centers of several of them contain supermassive black holes. Sagittarius A*, the name of the Milky Way's primary black hole, is four million times more massive than the Sun. GN-z11 is the oldest and furthest away galaxy as of March 2016. It can be seen as having existed only 400 million years after the Big Bang and is located 32 billion light-years away from Earth.

The majority of galaxies have diameters between 1,000 and 100,000 parsecs (or around 3,000 and 300,000 light years) and are spaced apart by millions of parsecs or more (or megaparsecs). For example, the distance between the Milky Way and its nearest massive neigh bour, the Andromeda Galaxy, which has a diameter of around 152,000 light years, is 780,000 parsecs, is at least 26,800 parsecs (87,400 light years) (2.5 million light year.)

The intergalactic medium, a thin gas with an average density of fewer than one atom per cubic meter, fills the space between galaxies. Most galaxies form groups, clusters, and superclusters through gravitational organization. The Milky Way is a member of the Local Group, which it and the Andromeda Galaxy dominate. A member of the Virgo Supercluster, the group. These relationships are typically organized into sheets and filaments at the greatest scale, encircled by enormous spaces. The Laniakea structure, a much bigger cosmic structure, contains both the Local Group and the Virgo Supercluster. Spiral nebulae were the name given to the first galaxies that were found by telescopy.

The majority of astronomers in the 18th and 19th centuries believed of them as either unresolved star clusters or nebulae and simply thought of them as being a part of the Milky Way, but their true makeup and natures remained a mystery. Larger telescope observations of a few neigh bouring bright galaxies, including the Andromeda Galaxy, started to resolve them into enormous star clusters, but the true distances of these objects placed them much beyond the Milky Way based only on the apparent faintness and sheer density of stars. They were referred regarded as island universes because of this, but this name quickly lost favour because the word universe meant the fullness of reality. Instead, they were referred to as just galaxies.

The 450–370 BCE Greek philosopher Democritus theorised that the Milky Way, a luminous band in the night sky, might actually be made up of far-off stars. The Milky Way, according to Aristotle, is the result of "the ignition of the fiery exhalation of some stars that were large, numerous, and close together," and the "ignition takes place in the upper part of the atmosphere, in the region of the World that is continuous with the heavenly motions." Olympiodorus the Younger, a Neoplatonist philosopher who lived from 495 to 570 CE, disagreed with this theory, claiming that the Milky Way should have parallax and appear differently depending on the time of day and location on Earth if it were sublunary (located between Earth and the Moon).

William Herschel began his first endeavour in 1785 to count the number of stars in various parts of the sky in order to explain the Milky Way's form and the Sun's position. He drew a picture of the galaxy's form, with the Solar System located in its center. Kapteyn in 1920 came to the image of a small (diameter roughly 15 kiloparsecs) ellipsoid galaxy with the Sun near to the center using a revised methodology. Harlow Shapley's alternative approach, which was based on the cataloguing of globular clusters, produced an entirely opposite result: a flat disc with a diameter of about 70 kiloparsecs and the Sun far from its core.

These systems display specific defining characteristics. They are figures of revolution with two equal primary axes because they exhibit perfect rotational symmetry. The alleged axis of rotation for them is a third, smaller axis.

Circular symmetry, a brilliant core encircled by a thin outer disc, and a superimposed spiral structure are the characteristics of spirals. They are separated into the conventional spirals and barred spirals parallel classes. The arms of regular spirals extend from the nucleus, but the arms of barred spirals extend from the ends of a bright, linear structure termed a bar that spans the nucleus. A spiral galaxy's nucleus is a sharply peaking region with a smooth texture. It can be fairly small or, in some situations, it can make up the majority of the galaxy. These galaxies appear to represent a bridge between the more prevalent elliptical and spiral galaxy types because they show certain characteristics of both. Long after his original categorization system had gained widespread acceptance, Hubble created the SO class, partly in response to the scarcity of severely flattened objects that otherwise exhibited the characteristics of elliptical galaxies. The traits mentioned here resulted from Sandage's expansion of the SO class.

SO galaxies are characterised by a smooth, featureless bulge and a faint outer envelope that encircle a brilliant centre. They are thin, with intrinsic minor to major axes ratios in the range of 0.1 to 0.3, according to statistical investigations of the ratio of the apparent axes (as seen projected onto the sky). Their structure often deviates from the luminosity law of elliptical galaxies and resembles spiral galaxies more. Some SO systems have a weak trace of structure in the envelope, either in the form of interstellar dust-produced narrow absorption lanes or faintly perceptible armlike discontinuities.

The narrow, tightly wound arms of these typical spirals are typically observable due to the presence of interstellar dust and, frequently, brilliant stars. The majority of them have a big amorphous bulge in the centre, but some of them defy this rule by having a small nucleus surrounded by an amorphous disc with thin, overlapping arms. The typical Sa galaxy is shown by NGC 1302, whereas the galaxy with a small nucleus and arms made up of thin dust lanes on a smooth disc is NGC 4866.

This transitional spiral type typically has a medium-sized core. Its shoulders are more spread out than the Sa variety and appear less smooth. They contain stars, star clouds, and interstellar gas and dust. Sb galaxies show wide variations in the details of their shape. For example, Hubble and Sandage observed that in some Sb galaxies the arms appear in a core that is often quite small. Other members of this subclass have arms that begin tangentially to a bright, nearly circular annulus, while others reveal a small, bright spiral pattern embedded in the nuclear bulge.

Hubble and Sandage noted further deviations from the established standard shapes for galaxies. Some systems have chaotic dust patterns superimposed on tightly coiled spiral arms. Some have thick, smooth arms with low surface luminosity, often surrounded by dust lines on their inner edges. Finally, there are those with a large, smooth nuclear bulge, from which the branches emanate, flowing tangentially to the bulge and forming short branch segments.

This is the most familiar type of galaxy and is best illustrated by the giant Andromeda galaxy. Many of these form changes are still mysterious. The basic shape of a Sb galaxy can be reproduced by theoretical spiral galaxy models based on a variety of hypotheses, but many of the above-noted variations are of relatively unexplained origin and must wait for more thorough and accurate modelling of galactic dynamics.

A very compact core and several open spiral arms with relatively high pitch angles are features common to these galaxies. The arms also have a lumpy appearance because to the abundance of irregularly distributed emission nebulae, stellar associations, star clusters, and star clouds that make up the star clouds. The systems can be divided into a number of distinct subtypes, just like   galaxies. Sandage lists the following six subdivisions: systems with multiple arms that start tangent to a bright ring centerd on the nucleus, those with arms that are poorly defined and span the entirety of the galaxy, those with spiral patterns that cannot be easily traced, that are numerous, and that are punctuated with chaotic dust. Galaxies with these characteristics include the Whirlpool Galaxy (M51), which has thin, branched arms that wind outward from a tiny nucleus and typically extend out about 180° before branching into multiple segments.

The final of the aforementioned subtypes is given its own categorization, type Sd, in some classification schemes, including that of the American astronomer Gerard de Vaucouleurs, who is of French descent. Additionally, it's been discovered that some of the fluctuations for Sc galaxies indicated here are connected to total luminosity. Galaxies of the first category are among the brightest spirals known, but galaxies of the fifth subtype typically have a tendency to be intrinsically faint.

Most members of this class are composed of highly irregular, gritty collections of light patches. They are often bluer in colour than the arms and discs of spiral galaxies and lack both visible symmetry and a clear core centre. However, just a few few of them are red and have a smooth, if asymmetrical, shape.

Irregular I and Irregular II are the two categories of irregular galaxies that Hubble identified. The Irr I type is the most prevalent of the irregular systems, and it appears to naturally occur when the spiral classes are extended beyond Sc into galaxies that lack any observable spiral structure. They are blue, have a little or no nucleus, and are well resolved. Systems are red, uncommon objects.

This group is no longer considered to be a viable way to categorized galaxies since it includes a variety of chaotic galaxies for which there appear to be many possible explanations, most frequently the outcomes of galaxy-galaxy interactions, including tidal distortions and cannibalism.

It took astronomers some time to figure out how to gauge the distances between galaxies before they could prove that they existed. It was previously described how, in the 1920s, astronomers made the first progress on this incredibly challenging assignment for the nearest galaxies. Up until the latter half of the 20th century, advancement was depressingly sluggish. Despite the fact that the issue was receiving more global attention, no agreement was reached. In actuality, the majority of researchers' findings could be divided into two groups, each of which had distances that were roughly twice as large as the others. The galaxy morphological classification is a method used by astronomers to categorized galaxies based on how they appear visually. Galaxies are categorized using a variety of methods based on their morphologies. The Hubble sequence, created by Edwin Hubble and later enhanced by Gerard Vaucouleurs and Allan Sandage, is the most well-known.

The disc of stars revolving around the bulge has a tendency to divide into arms that wrap around the galaxy. Numerous young stars are born in the regions of these spiral arms because they are rich in gas and dust. These budding stars have a brilliant brightness before they quickly fade away. The tightness of a spiral galaxy's spiral, the lumpiness of its arms, and the overall size of its centre bulge can all be used to categorise spiral galaxies.

Kardashev Scale

Based on how much energy a civilization can utilize, the Kardashev scale can be used to gauge its level of technical development. Soviet astronomer Nikolai Kardashev first proposed the measure in 1964.

The scale, which considers energy use on a cosmic scale, is hypothetical. Since then, a number of scale extensions have been proposed, including the use of metrics other than pure power and a larger range of power levels (types 0, IV to VI).

In a report delivered at the 1964 Byurakan conference, a scientific gathering that examined the Soviet radio astronomy space listening program, Kardashev first described his scale. This article, titled "Transmission of Information by Extraterrestrial Civilizations" (later translated as "Transmission of Information by Extraterrestrial Civilizations"), makes the case for a three-type classification of civilizations based on the idea of exponential growth. A civilization of type I is able to access all the energy on its planet and store it for later use. A type II civilization can use a star's energy directly.

A type III civilization can eventually absorb all of the energy released by its galaxy. In a second piece from the same year, "Strategies of Searching for Extraterrestrial Intelligence," Kardashev speculates on civilization, which he defines as the ability to get energy, sustain itself, and incorporate data from its surroundings.

The Soviet astronomer suggests ways to find supercivilizations and to guide SETI program in the next two publications, "On the Inevitability and the Possible Structure of Supercivilizations" and "Cosmology and Civilizations," which were published in 1985 and 1997, respectively. Two major re-evaluations of Kardashev's scale have been conducted: Carl

Sagan's refinement of the types and Michio Kaku's rejection of the energy postulate in favour of the knowledge economy.

Numerous authors have been able to challenge Kardashev's original classification and either complete it or deny it as a result of other debates over the nature of the various categories. Thus, two opposing critical viewpoints have developed: one that challenges Kardashev's postulates and considers them to be insufficient or inconsistent, and the other that proposes alternative scales. Numerous scenarios investigating the prospect of more advanced civilizations have been inspired by the Kardashev scale. During the conference conducted in 1964 in Armenia at the Byurakan astrophysical observatory, the framework for the search for and detection of advanced civilizations was built and theorised.

The initial Kardashev model was developed using a functional definition of civilization that was based on the immutability of physical principles and used human civilization as an extrapolation model.

Several scientists have made numerous attempts to find potential civilizations, but without success. These standards led to the identification of strange objects that are now known to be either pulsars or quasars. Kardashev has outlined a set of listening and watching parameters to be taken into consideration in his numerous works; however, other authors, most notably Samouel Aronovitch Kaplan and Guillermo A. Lemarchand, believe that these are insufficient and need to be supplemented. According to the two criteria of access and use of energy, the Kardashev scale, an illustrative classification, divides civilizational evolution into three stages. This classification assumes that a portion of the energy consumed by each kind is meant for communication with other civilizations, and is used to direct the search for extraterrestrial civilizations, particularly within SETI, in which Kardashev contributed. Lemarchand compares the speed of transmission across the galaxy of a volume of information similar to a medium-sized library to help us better appreciate its scale.

There are numerous instances in history of human civilization going through significant changes, like the Industrial Revolution. Since the transition between Kardashev scale levels entails exceeding the strict limits of the resources accessible in a civilization's existing region, they may potentially represent similarly violent moments of societal upheaval.

According to a frequent theory, the shift from Type 0 to Type I could involve a significant risk of self-destruction because, in some cases, the civilization's home planet might become inhospitable to future expansion, as in the case of a Malthusian catastrophe. For instance, it is conceivable that excessive energy use without sufficient heat disposal may render the planet of a civilization on the cusp of Type I unfit for the biology of the dominant life-forms and their food sources.

If Earth serves as an example, water temperatures beyond 35 °C (95 °F) would endanger marine life and make it difficult, if not impossible, to cool mammals to degrees that are adequate for their metabolism. Of course, future technical and technological developments may prevent these theoretical conjectures from materializing as issues.

A civilization may colonize neigh bour worlds or established O'Neill-style colonies by the time it reaches Type I, allowing waste heat to be dispersed across the planetary system. It has also grown to be hard to accept that the Kardashev scale uses unlimited development as a gauge of advancement. Ivanov said that it had its origins in the radio astronomers' preeminence of SETI at the time. "Bigger is better for radio astronomers," he declared. For them, increased power logically indicated a more developed culture. But since the effects of humans' use of fossil fuels on the planet have grown more apparent over time, it is no longer safe to idealise steady energy consumption.

The central conflict in the ongoing search for extraterrestrial life is also addressed in Kardashev's paper: is it more important to look for technology signatures, such as radio waves, which depend on intelligent life with developed technologies, as opposed to biosignatures, which are changes to a planet that only life at some scale, such as microbes and manatees, can cause?

However, despite the fact that Kardashev's study is solely concerned with technology signatures, it acknowledges the biosignature side as well and makes the case that one search can help with the other. He wrote: "The possibility that multiple type II civilizations exist in the galaxy would be significantly increased by the discovery of even the most basic species, on Mars for example." Of course, a significant role for radio astronomical searches in solving this issue. Kardashev's classification system was not based on social or ethical systems because we will probably never foresee such things about alien civilizations. Instead, it was built on energy, a concept that anyone with a background in physics will find to be quite meaningful. Because a civilization cannot be built without energy, energy consumption may serve as the foundation for universal stages of civilization progression. Kardashev therefore used the energy sources that were available to civilizations as they advanced technologically to construct his scale.

Type 1: The first stage consists of civilizations that can utilize all the energy sources on their home planet. This would entail collecting all of the light energy that a world receives from its star. This makes sense given that the primary energy source on the majority of worlds where life may exist would be stars. For instance, the Sun provides the Earth with energy equivalent to hundreds of atomic bombs per second. That is a pretty significant source of energy, and a Type 1 species would have access to it all to develop civilizations.

Type 2: These societies are able to fully utilize their home star's energy resources. Kardashev's ideas on this were famously anticipated by Nobel Prize-winning scientist Freeman Dyson, who envisioned a highly developed civilization creating a massive sphere around its star. A device the size of the entire solar system called a "Dyson Sphere" would be used to collect stellar photons and their energy. Type 3: The energy produced by every star in their home galaxy may be used by these super-civilizations.

There is a lot of energy involved in the few hundred billion stars that make up a typical galaxy. There might be more advanced techniques as well, such as having the civilization surround every star in their galaxy with Dyson spheres. We move from the imaginable to the god-like as we move up the Type 1 scale. It is not difficult to conceive, for instance, utilizing a large number of enormous satellites in orbit to collect solar energy and then beaming that energy down to Earth via microwaves. That would advance us to a civilization of type 1.

However, devouring entire planets would be necessary to create a Dyson sphere. How long till we get power like that? How would we need to alter our route to get there? Once we reach Type 3 civilizations, we almost begin to imagine divine beings capable of designing entire galaxies.

Mars Colonization

The idea of human migration to Mars and permanent human habitation there is known as "colonization" or "settlement" of Mars. Public space agencies and commercial enterprises are both interested in the idea, and science fiction literature, film, and art have all extensively explored it. The first stage in any colony project would be a human expedition to Mars, but no one has ever visited the planet, and there have been no resupply missions either. Landers and rovers, on the other hand, have successfully investigated the planet's surface and transmitted data on the local environment.

The asteroid belt and the Earth's orbit are both near to Mars' orbit. Although Mars'day and general makeup resemble Earth's, the planet is inhospitable to life. Although Mars' average temperature varies between 94 and 32 °F (70 and 0 °C), its unbreathable atmosphere is thick enough to produce planet-wide dust storms. Ionizing radiation is severe, and fine dust blankets the arid Martian surface. Colonists on Mars might take advantage of in-situ resources such subterranean water, Martian soil, and minerals. On Mars, there are few opportunities to produce electricity utilising nuclear, solar, or wind energy. Curiosity, the ability for people to conduct more in-depth observational study than unmanned rovers, a financial interest in its resources, and the chance that human extinction may be lowered by colonizing other planets are some of the justifications and motives for colonizing Mars.

Risks and challenges include exposure to radiation while visiting Mars and while on its surface, toxic soil, low gravity, the isolation brought about by Mars' separation from Earth, a lack of water, and chilly temperatures. Compared to Earth, Mars' surface gravity is only 38% greater. It is unknown if Martian gravity would have a similar impact to microgravity in terms of health issues like muscle loss and bone demineralization.

Lack of finance forced the cancellation of the Mars Gravity Biosatellite project, which was intended to find out more about how Mars' lower surface gravity will affect humans. Mars has a surface area that is 28.4% of Earth's, just shy of Earth's dry land, which makes up 29.2% of Earth's surface.

Mars has one-tenth the mass and half the radius of Earth. This indicates that it is less dense on average and has a smaller volume than Earth. To aid in the ultimate colonization of Mars, SpaceX has suggested creating a transportation system on Mars.

The mission architecture consists of fully reusable launch vehicles, human-rated spacecraft, on-orbit propellant tankers, quick launch/landing platforms, and on-site resource utilization for local rocket fuel generation on Mars (ISRU). As of 2017, SpaceX's aspirational objective was to land the first two crewed starships by 2026 and its cargo starships on Mars by 2024. Although Mars is about 52% further from the Sun, only around 43.3% of the solar energy that reaches the Earth's higher atmosphere per unit area (the solar constant) enters Mars' upper atmosphere.

A bigger percentage of the solar energy does, however, reach the surface as radiation because of the much thinner atmosphere. Optimal circumstances on the Martian equator are comparable to those on Devon Island in the Canadian Arctic in June; the maximum solar irradiation on Mars is approximately 590 W/m2 compared to approximately 1000 W/m2 at the Earth's surface. The more eccentric Mars' orbit is compared to Earth's, which causes temperature and solar constant changes to rise over the course of a Martian year. [Reference needed] There are almost no clouds and no precipitation on Mars. Earth has regions that humans have investigated that resemble some Martian conditions.

According to NASA rover data, the temperatures on Mars are comparable to those in Antarctica at low latitudes. The maximum heights reached by manned balloon ascents (35 km

(114,000 feet) in 1961 and 38 km in 2012) have air pressure that is comparable to that of Mars' surface.

The pilots, however, were seated in a pressurized capsule instead of being exposed to the extremely low pressure, which would have killed them. Living in elaborate manmade Mars homes with sophisticated life-support systems would be necessary for human survival on Mars. Water processing systems would be a crucial component of this. A human being, which is primarily composed of water, would perish in a matter of days without it. Dizziness and weariness are brought on by even a 5-8% drop in total body water, while physical and mental damage is brought on by a 10% drop (See Dehydration). In the UK, an individual uses, on average, 70 to 140 litres of water per day. Through practice and education, astronauts on the ISS have demonstrated that far less can be used and that the water recovery systems on the ISS can recycle about 70% of what is used.

Gravitational differences may harm human health by weakening bones and muscles. Cardiovascular issues and osteoporosis are also possible risks. The International Space Station's current rotations keep humans in zero gravity for six months, which is about the same as a round-trip to Mars. This enables researchers to comprehend the physical state that Mars-bound astronauts might arrive in more fully. Surface gravity on Mars is only 38% of that on Earth.

The cardiovascular, musculoskeletal, and neurovestibular (central nerve) systems are all impacted by microgravity. The consequences on the heart are intricate. In microgravity, the blood does not stay 70% below the heart as it does on Earth because there is nothing to pull the blood down.

This may lead to a number of unfavourable outcomes. The blood pressure in the legs and lower body is much lower once in microgravity. Legs weaken as a result from the loss of bone and muscle mass.

Astronauts exhibit symptoms of chicken legs syndrome and a swollen face. Blood samples taken during the first day of re-entering the atmosphere revealed a 17% loss of blood plasma, which was a factor in the fall of erythropoietin secretion. Long space flights and exposure to microgravity promote demineralization and muscle atrophy in the skeletal system, which is crucial for maintaining our body's posture. Astronauts were seen to experience a wide range of symptoms during re-acclimation, including cold chills, nausea, vomiting, and motion sickness.

Returning astronauts experienced similar confusion. Despite Mars' greater distance from the Sun than Earth, dangerous radiation levels still reach the surface. Since Mars no longer has an inner dynamo, it has a weaker global magnetosphere than Earth. This makes it possible for a large amount of ionising radiation to reach the Martian surface when combined with a thin atmosphere. Galactic cosmic rays (GCR) and solar energetic particles are the two main radiation dangers when venturing beyond of Earth's atmosphere and magnetosphere (SEP).

The atmosphere shields the planet from uncharged, extremely energetic GCRs, while the magnetosphere shields it from charged particles from the Sun. Mars is the only planet, aside from Venus, whose distance from Earth takes the least amount of energy per unit mass.

A voyage to Mars takes around nine months in space using a Hohmann transfer orbit. With incrementally higher amounts of energy and fuel compared to a Hohmann transfer orbit, modified transfer trajectories that reduce the distance travelled to four to seven months in space are feasible and are routinely used for robotic Mars missions. With chemical rockets, it is challenging to reduce the travel time below six months because it calls for larger delta-v and a growing amount of fuel. Advanced spaceship propulsion systems, some of which have previously undergone varied degrees of testing, such as nuclear rockets and the Variable Specific Impulse Magneto plasma Rocket, may make it possible. A trip lasting forty days may be made in the first scenario, and a trip lasting only two weeks or so in the second. A scientist from the University of California, Santa Barbara claimed in 2016 that the use of a laser propelled sail (directed photonic propulsion) system instead of a fuel-based rocket propulsion system could further reduce the travel time for a small robotic probe to Mars down to "as little as 72 hours." Mars' atmosphere has a density of around 0.6% of Earth's and has a surface gravity that is 0.38 times that of Earth. It is challenging to land heavy, crewed spacecraft with only thrusters, as was done with the Apollo Moon landings, due to the relatively strong gravity and the presence of aerodynamic effects. However, the atmosphere is too thin for aerodynamic effects to be of much assistance in aerobraking and landing a large vehicle. The braking and landing mechanisms needed to land manned missions on Mars would be different from those for robotic missions or crewed spacecraft on the Moon. The colony would require the essential services required to support human civilization in order to operate at all. These would have to be built to withstand the hostile Martian environment and either have to be used while wearing an EVA suit or housed in a place that is suitable for people to live in. For instance, if solar energy is used to generate electricity, massive energy storage facilities will also be required to cover the times when dust storms obstruct the sun. Additionally, automatic dust removal systems may be required to protect people from the conditions on the surface.

Systems must maximize the utilization of local resources if the colony is to grow beyond a small number of residents in order to minimize the requirement for resupply from Earth. During the half-sol, when Earth is over the Martian horizon, communication with Earth is quite simple.

Several of, Mars orbiters built by NASA and ESA have communications relay equipment, indicating that Mars already has satellite communications. Even though they will eventually break down, more orbiters with the potential to serve as communication relays will probably be launched before any colonization efforts are mounted. The one-way communication delay caused by the speed of light varies from around 3 minutes at closest approach (estimated by the difference between Mars' perihelion and Earth's aphelion), to 22 minutes at the closest superior conjunction (approximated by aphelion of Mars plus aphelion of Earth). Due to the significant time gaps involved, real-time communication between Earth and Mars would be exceedingly impracticable, such as phone calls or Internet Relay Chat.

Around the time of superior conjunction, when the Sun is directly between Mars and Earth, NASA has discovered that direct communication can be cut off for about two weeks every synodic period. However, the actual length of the communications blackout varies from mission to mission depending on various factors, such as the amount of link margin built into the communications system and the minimum data rate that is acceptable from a mission standpoint.

In actuality, the majority of Mars missions have experienced communication blackouts for up to a month at a time. Robotic systems like the Mars Exploration Rovers Spirit, Opportunity, Curiosity, and Perseverance could pave the way for a human settlement. These technologies might be used to find resources that would support the development and well-being of a colony, such as ice or ground water. These systems would last for years or perhaps decades, and as recent advancements in commercial spaceflight have proven, it's possible that both private and public ownership will be present.

In addition, these robotic technologies are less expensive and political risky than early crewed operations. By producing different consumables including fuel, oxidizers, water, and building materials, wired systems may establish the basis for early crewed landings and bases.

Space Exploration

The study and exploration of space, which includes looking for new celestial bodies and creating new technology to make this kind of research possible, is referred to as space exploration. It is an intriguing area that combines science, engineering, and exploratory components and has resulted in numerous important scientific and technological advancements.

After the Soviet Union launched Sputnik, the first artificial satellite, in 1957, the history of space exploration began to take off. Since then, space exploration has substantially increased as multiple government and private organizations have created and launched a wide range of spacecraft for various uses.

Among the main objectives of space exploration are: Understanding the universe's origins and development, looking for signs of life on other planets and space objects, study and mapping of celestial objects such planets, moons, and asteroids, developing innovative space travel technologies and capabilities, such as reusable rockets and cutting-edge propulsion systems conducting scientific studies in the exceptional environment of space, such as examining how the human body responds to microgravity.

The creation of new materials and technologies, improvement of weather forecasting and communication systems, and more knowledge of the Earth's ecosystem and climate are just a few of the many practical advantages that space exploration has brought about. Multiple significant scientific advancements have resulted from space exploration, including the discovering of water on the Moon and Mars, the identification of numerous exoplanets, and the investigation of the universe's early development and history. Additionally, it has led to a great deal of technological advancements, including GPS, satellite communication, improved materials, and propulsion systems.

With the Soviet Union's Sputnik 1 spacecraft entering orbit in 1957, humankind has been exploring space for a very long time. Numerous missions to explore the solar system and beyond, both manned and unmanned, have been launched since then. These missions were conducted by a number of space agencies, including NASA (United States), the European Space Agency (ESA), and the Russian Federal Space Agency (Roscosmos).

Our comprehension of the universe has greatly benefited from space research, which has also sparked many technical developments on Earth. Additionally, it has stimulated interest in space exploration and astronomy among the general population and encouraged people to pursue jobs in STEM fields (science, technology, engineering, and math).

The cost of launching spacecraft and the risks of space flight is just two of the numerous difficulties and dangers that come with space exploration. But many nations and organization are studying and exploring it because of the potential benefits— both scientific and technical. Even while astronomy, or the study of celestial objects, has existed since the beginning of trustworthy written history, it wasn't until the mid-20th century rocket development boom that the possibility of physical space exploration became a reality. The Opel-RAK program, run by Fritz von Opel and Max Valier in the late 1920s, produced the first crewed rocket vehicles and rocket planes. This effort laid the way for the Nazi era V2 program as well as US and Soviet activity from 1950 onward. The Opel-RAK program, as well as the spectacular public vehicle displays that attracted vast crowds and created the "Rocket Rumble" phenomenon, had a profound and long-lasting influence on future space pioneers.

People have always regarded the heavens and pondered the nature of the celestial bodies seen in the night sky. In the 20th century, technology advancements in electronics, other fields, and the creation of rockets made it possible to launch machines, animals, and eventually humans into space.

But even before technology made these accomplishments possible, many people—including scientists, writers, and artists—were fascinated by the idea of exploring space. By achieving spaceflight, humanity was able to explore the solar system and the rest of the cosmos, comprehend the numerous objects and phenomena that are more easily viewed from space, and take advantage of the resources and characteristics of the space environment for their own profit. Discovery, scientific knowledge, and the use of that knowledge to further human objectives are all aspects of space exploration. (See spaceflight for more information about spacecraft in general, launch considerations, flight trajectories, and navigation, docking, and recovery processes.

Although people from all walks of life have long been intrigued by the prospect of exploring space, only national governments were able to bear the exorbitant expenditures of sending humans and machines into space for the majority of the latter mid - twentieth century and the early 21st century. Due to this reality, exploration of space had to advance a wide range of interests, which it has done in a number of different ways. The public has benefited greatly from government space initiatives, which have advanced knowledge, served as markers of nation power and prestige improved national security, and strengthened military capabilities.

Institutions, philanthropic institutions, and other nongovernmental donors had previously supported research that enhanced fundamental understanding about nature, but in the years following World War II, governments took the lead in doing so. There were two causes for this alteration. First off, only governments could pay the costs associated with the big teams of researchers who needed specialized equipment to conduct numerous scientific investigations. Second, governments agreed to shoulder this burden because they thought fundamental research would result in new information vital to the safety, security, and general well-being of their people.

When scientists sought government support for early space experiments, it was forthcoming. Since the start of space efforts in the United States, the Soviet Union, and Europe, national governments have given high priority to the support of science done in and from space. From modest beginnings, space science has expanded under government support to include multibillion-dollar exploratory missions in the solar system.

Examples of such efforts include the development of the Curiosity Mars rover, the Cassini-Huygens mission to Saturn and its moons, and the development of major space-based astronomical observatories such as the Hubble Space Telescope.

Soviet leader Nikita Khrushchev in 1957 used the fact that his country had been first to launch a satellite as evidence of the technological power of the Soviet Union and of the superiority of communism. The daily lives of several people on Earth have benefited from and continue to benefit from the vital services that orbiting satellites have offered. Information on both long-term and short-term weather patterns, as well as their underlying causes, is provided by meteorologic satellites. Other Earth-observation satellites use remote sensing to obtain information about land and ocean areas.

This information is used to better manage Earth's resources and to better understand how the climate is changing. Communications satellites provide virtually immediate voice, image, and data transmission on a worldwide scale. Many terrestrial users depend on the precise navigation, positioning, and timing data provided by satellites controlled by the United States, Russian, China, Japan, India, and Europe. Other nations have followed the Soviets and the United States in creating their own space program as the many advantages of space activities have come to light. Along with China, Japan, Canada, India, Israel, Iran, North Korea, South Korea, and Brazil, these nations operate both independently and jointly through the European Space Agency. Several western European nations are also among them.

More than 50 nations have private space companies or other governmental organizations engaged in space activities by the middle decade of the twenty-first century.

Since 1957, robotic spacecraft and Earth-orbiting satellites have gathered important information on the Sun, Earth, other solar system entities, and the universe beyond. Robotic spacecraft have visited all of the major planets, landed on the Moon, Venus, Mars, Titan, a comet, four asteroids, and flown past Kuiper belt objects and comet nuclei, including Halley's Comet, as they traverse through the inner solar system. Scientists have improved our knowledge of the creation and evolution of galaxies, stars, planets, and other cosmic phenomena using data from space.

Appendix

End of Universe

The eventual outcome of the universe is a subject in big bang cosmology, whose theoretical constraints allow for the description and assessment of several possibilities for the evolution and final fate of the universe. Determining the fate and evolution of the cosmos has emerged as a legitimate cosmological topic based on empirical evidence, transcending the mostly untestable confines of mythological or theological ideas. Different scientific ideas have projected a variety of potential outcomes, such as the possibility that the cosmos may have existed for both an infinite and a finite amount of time, or towards describing the way and conditions of its creation.

The idea of a static cosmos was shared by Einstein and his contemporaries. When Einstein discovered that it was simple to solve his general relativity equations in a way that would allow the universe to be expanding at the moment and contracting in the far coming years, he added to those calculations what he called a cosmological constant—basically, a constant energy density that is unaffected by any expansion or contraction—whose purpose was to counteract the effect of gravity on the spiritual realm as a whole in order to keep the universe static. Einstein would later claim that his uncertainty principle was "the greatest folly of my life" once Hubble revealed that the cosmos was expanding.

In the hypothetical scenario known as "The Big Crunch," the universe's expansion would ultimately come to an end and the cosmos would collapse, reducing the astronomical scale factor to zero. A different Big Bang could occur after this one, re-creating the cosmos. The vast majority of the current data contradicts this theory. However, astronomical studies show that the universe is expanding faster than it is slowing down because of gravity, suggesting that the universe is significantly likely to end in heat death.

The future of the cosmos can be predicted by observing which of two forces—gravity and the bursting force first from Big Bang—will prevail. The Big Crunch will begin, reversing initial Big Bang, if gravity is able to outweigh the destructive power of the Big Bang; but, if it failed, heat death is the most likely outcome. Astronomers are aware that the expanding universe is but they are unsure of the exact magnitude of the extension force.

When this radiation is condensed and blue shifted to higher energies, it becomes intense enough to ignite the surface of stars before they collide. The end of the Big Crunch would've been filled with radiation from stars and high-energy particles.

According to the Big Crunch theory, the universe's overall matter density is so great that gravitational pull will eventually triumph over the Big Bang's initial expansion. The average fuel density, Hubble constant, and cosmological constant can all be used by the FLRW cosmology to determine that whether expansion will finally come to an end. If the rate of metric expansion were to stop, contraction would unavoidably follow, speeding up over time and bringing the cosmos to an end through a form of gravitational collapse that would turn the entire galaxy into a black hole.

There are other more recent speculations of circular universes. According to Paul Steinhardt's Ekpyrotic theory, the Big Bang may have resulted from the collision of two simultaneous orbifold planes, known as branes, in a region of higher dimensions. A brace is where the four-dimensional universe is located. Following the collision, there will be a Big Bang. Quantum fluctuations from a time before branes are present in the materials and radiation that surround us today. The cosmos has attained its current state after many billions of years, and after another few billions of years it will begin to contract. The flatness and monopole in the earlier theories can be fixed because dark energy correlates to the force between the two branes.

Constellations

An area of the celestial sphere known as a constellation is one in which a collection of discernible stars appears to create a pattern or outline, generally resembling an animal, mythological figure, or inanimate object.

The first constellations probably have their origins in prehistoric times. They were used by people to share tales about their beliefs, encounters, creations, or mythology. Before the current constellations were acknowledged worldwide, various cultures and nations adopted their own constellations, some of which persisted into the first decade of the 20th century. Over time, there have been substantial changes in how constellations are recognized. Many had size or shape changes. Others rose to fame just to fade into obscurity. Some were restricted to a particular culture or country.

Greek constellations make up the conventional Western 48. They are mentioned in Phenomena by Aratus and Ptolemy's Almagest, despite the fact that their original publication dates from several centuries before these works. From the 15th century to the middle of the 18th century, when European explorers started visiting the Southern Hemisphere, constellation in the far southern sky were added. The zodiac consists of twelve (or thirteen) ancient constellations (straddling the ecliptic, which the Sun, Moon, and planets all traverse). The zodiac's historical beginnings are still unknown; nevertheless, its astrological divisions first emerged in Babylonian or Chaldean astrology around 400 BC.

While not quite constellations according to the strict definition, other star patterns or groups known as asterisms are still employed by observers to find their way across the night sky. Asterisms can consist of multiple stars in a single constellation or they might include stars from multiple constellations.

1) Ursa Minor

This constellation usually depicts a tiny bear with a long tail, at the exact tip of the tail there lies the pole star which is also known as Polaris. Polaris is considered as the brightest star in the constellation Ursa minor. It is also classified as little dipper because its main stars look like a smaller version of the big dipper which is present in the constellation Ursa Major. This constellation is found when it was the period of ancient Greeks.

2)Ursa Major

This is one of largest constellation which is seen in the night sky. In. which it represents seven brightest stars. It is near the big dipper which is one of the best-known features in whole sky. There are two farthest stars in this constellation which are Merak and Dubhe. They are also known as the pointers of the pole star.

3)Lynx

This is very faint constellation and very hard to detect with naked eyes in sky. This constellation is trapped in between Ursa Major and Auriga. Lynx is a combination of double and triple star systems which can also be detected and studied by small telescope.

4) Hercules

This constellation is named after Hercules, who was the strongest in Greek mythology. It is depicting brandishing a club. And also depicts a dragon, situated on the top of his head, which he killed himself. The stars in the constellations are not bright enough thus hard to find in the night sky. The main feature of this constellation is square shape of stars.

5)Cygnus

The ancient Greeks visualized Cygnus as the swan flying alone Milky Way. Deneb is its brightest star in sky. In mythology, the swan was the disguise used by the god Zeus when he visited Queen Leda of Sparta. The overall shape of the constellation resembles a large cross. One of the most important feature of Cygnus lies in the neck of the swan, which is a black hole.

6)Andromeda

This constellation is named after a princess of Greek mythology who was chained to a rock by her parents. She was rescued by hero Perseus who lies next her in the sky. In ancient times star named Alpheratz was shared with the constellation Pegasus.

Time Travel

It is unknown whether going back in time is scientifically possible, and if it is, there may be causality issues that arise. It has been widely seen and is generally understood within the context of special relativity and general relativity to be possible to move through time in the opposite direction from how we typically perceive it.

With current technology, it is not possible to make one body advance or delay another body by more beyond a few milliseconds. Space travel into the past and future may be conceivable under certain conditions, according to several theories, notably famously special and general relativity, if certain spacetime geometries or motions exist. Physicists speculate about the idea of closed time-like curves—world lines that create closed loops in spacetime and permit objects to travel back in time—in technical publications.

There are known solutions to the general relativity equations that describe spacetimes with closed time series curves, such as the Gödel spacetime, however it is unclear how physically plausible these solutions are.